# MARY DEMUTH

# NOT
# MARKED

## FINDING HOPE & HEALING AFTER
## SEXUAL ABUSE

Uncaged Publishing

Not Marked by Mary DeMuth
Copyright 2013 by Mary DeMuth
Published by Uncaged Publishing
Rockwall, TX 75087
www.marydemuth.com

Cover Design by Loc Le, Ho Chi Minh City, Vietnam

This book contains stories in which the author has changed people's names and some details of their situations in order to protect their privacy.

Library of Congress Cataloguing-in-Publication Data
DeMuth, Mary E. 1967-

    Not Marked/Mary DeMuth
    p. cm.
    Includes biographical references
    ISBN (pbk.) 978-0-9834367-7-5
    ISBN (eBook) 978-0-9834367-8-2
    1. Christian Living 2. Memoir

Printed in the United States of America.

# ENDORSEMENTS FOR *NOT MARKED*

*"There is no one I trust more than Mary to come alongside those wounded by sexual abuse and then, with gentleness and compassion and strength, breathe hope and healing into their souls. Mary knows her stuff, absolutely, but what sets her apart is her deep love for Jesus, and her faith-filled commitment to seeing wholeness and healing become a reality for people who have suffered from sexual abuse. This book will bring healing and hope to so many."*

SARAH BESSEY, AUTHOR OF *JESUS FEMINIST*

*"Silence and shame are nobody's friends. This book is many things, including a brutal but beautiful account of one woman's path to healing. But for me, it's a reminder to open my mouth. Thank you, Mary, for going first—for speaking up on behalf of those whose voices need to be heard."*

JEFF GOINS, AUTHOR OF
*THE IN-BETWEEN: EMBRACING THE TENSION
BETWEEN NOW AND THE NEXT BIG THING*

"Mary's bravery is essential in a day when 1 in 4 women have suffered abuse. This project was not optional, it was a calling and God will use it to heal many women, who feel alone."

JENNIE ALLEN, AUTHOR OF *ANYTHING*

"Mary has written a courageous book about her journey healing from sexual abuse. She is raw, authentic, and encouraging. Anyone who is a survivor of sexual abuse will not feel alone but will relate to so many of Mary and Patrick's struggles. You can hear her hope and the truth about God's presence in healing. You will be touched by her strength and fierce grip on God's steadfast hand, to overcome and replace the lies of the enemy with God's truth and love."

CAROLYN SIDEREAS M.S., LPC-S,
DIRECTOR OF LAKE POINTE CHURCH COUNSELING,
ROCKWALL, TEXAS

"A brutally candid but elegant unveiling penned by one of today's foremost Christian authors. If you've suffered any kind of abuse in life, Mary's superb new book will lead you by the hand to the world's greatest Healer who knows exactly how to restore your heart and set you free from guilt, shame, and bitterness."

FRANK VIOLA, AUTHOR OF
*GOD'S FAVORITE PLACE ON EARTH*

"As a counselor it's often difficult to ask someone to walk the painful path to healing from childhood sexual abuse. I know it's the path to freedom, but the journey often feels lonely and frightening. Thanks to Mary DeMuth's wise and courageous book I can say to a client, 'Read this and you won't feel so alone. Mary has a map and she will make the trip with you.'"

CHUCK ROBERTS, M.A., LPC, MANAGING DIRECTOR
CENTER FOR BIBLICAL COUNSELING,
MCKINNEY, TEXAS

"Mary's advice regarding sexual intimacy in marriage is applicable even for those who haven't suffered abuse, and her hard-won wisdom is underscored and enhanced by husband Patrick's helpful insights, as he honestly shares the struggles and responsibilities of a sex-abuse victim's spouse. Their journey as a couple reveals an important truth: Darkness flees before light, but first we have to let the light in, and that means revisiting the dark places. The good news? We don't go alone. Jesus goes with us, and He not only reveals and redefines reality, He redeems it, beautifying even the deepest scars. This book is a road map to restoration and real joy. I hope it finds its way into the hands of those who need it, and I pray the Healer meets them on the pages."

JEANNE DAMOFF, AUTHOR AND SPEAKER

"Divinely inspired words that will heal your heart, give you the steps to be redeemed from your past, and offer you hope. You can't read this book and walk away unchanged."

SUNDI JO GRAHAM, SPEAKER, AUTHOR, AND FOUNDER OF ESTHER'S HOUSE OF REDEMPTION

"I find Not Marked to be a most powerful read. Mary DeMuth, an in-the-trenches-with-you author, comes with a fractured past, yet the healing she has found since is what covers the pages. I love the idea that broken people will read this book and find community. I love, most, that they will read it and find hope."

LISA WHITTLE, AUTHOR OF WHOLE

"A raw and brave sojourn into the difficult—but possible—work of healing from childhood sexual abuse, Not Marked should be a top resource on counselor and pastoral shelves, as well as in the homes of survivors. A welcome, no holds barred, Christian perspective into the realities survivors face on the road toward discovering hope and freedom."

AMY K. SORRELLS, AUTHOR OF HOW SWEET THE SOUND

"Not sure you can (or want to) trust your 'marked' heart, body, soul, and story to yet one more, perhaps, unknown author? Read and discover for yourself the heart and bold intentionality of honesty which Mary brings to the page for your good. This, coupled with the interspersed observations of her husband, makes for a powerfully written instrument of Not Marked change."

JULIE BARNHILL, AUTHOR AND SPEAKER,

WWW.JULIEBARNHILL.COM

"Your story is not over. If you are holding this book, the chances are you know someone whose sense of worth has been stolen by senseless sexual acts. Maybe it's happened to you. If you were the one hurt, know that you are not alone. Those words may comfort you and cause your heart to hurt more. But dear one, you are far from alone. Not Marked is Mary's story. Like far too many of you, she's been hurt badly. Stories of hurt aren't easy to read or write. As Mary bravely recounts the journey, my prayer is that you, O Beloved Child of God, find healing as well. Because your story is not over."

CAITLIN MUIR, FLAWED JESUS FOLLOWER,

STORYTELLER, AND FRIEND.

WWW.CAITLINMUIR.COM

"Just. Wow. This it a brave work that does more than merely bringing a candle into the darkness. Rather it brings a 100,000 lumens spotlight in and demands that we see the issue of sexual abuse in plain daylight. Better yet, it shines on the healing and hope that can be found in a Christ whose heart breaks at the pain suffered by so many victims. I applaud Mary for using her story and experience to bring the same redemption for others."

DAN KING, SPEAKER AND CO-AUTHOR OF
*ACTIVIST FAITH: FROM HIM AND FOR HIM*

"It's so difficult to hear about how my friend Mary was abused and victimized, but I'm so grateful Mary wrote this book. It is a tool for those who have been abused, but it's also a tool for people like me who want to help friends but don't know how. Mary's husband's contribution to this book is particularly important for spouses of victims. I was moved by his words as much as I was moved by hers."

ANDY TRAUB, AUTHOR AND PODCASTER

One of the things I esteem in Mary DeMuth is the generosity with which she shares her story. 2 Corinthians tells us, after we've received comfort from God in our own dark journeys and come out on the other side, we—in the same way this God of comfort comforted us—can then comfort others who struggle under their own weight of pain. *Not Marked* is Mary's gift of encouragement to you, a result of Mary experiencing, first-hand, a brand new freedom in Christ.

DEIDRA RIGGS, MANAGING EDITOR,

THEHIGHCALLING.ORG

"Mary DeMuth has guts. This book took a great amount of courage and surrender to write, and by her example of bold honesty, Mary is giving others permission to tell their own stories of abuse. But she is also holding up a torch to light the path to healing, as she demonstrates that the trauma of abuse is not the end of the story. There is healing in the love of Jesus, and, having experienced it bit by bit over years of walking in the light of that love, it is as if she is now taking each reader by the hand and guiding them to Him, so that they may be healed as well."

CHRISTY TENNANT KRISPIN,

WRITER/ACTOR/MUSICIAN

*For all those who feel marked, tainted,*
*and unnecessary on this earth:*
*I hope you close this book cleansed,*
*renewed, and wholly loved,*
*living an umarked story.*

# TABLE OF CONTENTS

# A CAVEAT

*"The sovereign Lord has given me His words of wisdom,*

*so that I know how to comfort the weary."*

ISAIAH 50:4, ESV

I am not a psychologist. I hold no counseling degrees or certificates, though I've scoured many sexual abuse books written by counselors. I don't write this book as though I were a counselor. It is not a sterile healing manual or a proven method. My hope is that in simply telling my story, you will find some gouges I've made in the rock to use as footholds as you climb your way toward health. May you, perhaps for the very first time, understand this powerful truth: you are not alone. And when the days seem especially dark, when you feel like you're forever marked and doomed to darkness, you'll pick up this book again and remind yourself that you are in the midst of God's restoration process. I wish you healing. I wish you light. And as I type these words, I can't help but start this book with prayer.

1

Dear, dear Jesus. Please surround my friend reading this book with peace. Take away the fear that rumbles inside. Remove the panic. Slow the racing heart. Silence the maniacal voices that shout unworthiness, dirtiness, and shame. Would You please begin a new, vital healing journey even right now in this moment? I believe You long to set all Your sons and daughters free from what happened in the darkness. On the cross You crushed the schemes of the evil one, who comes to steal, kill, and destroy. May it be that we realize afresh that You, naked on that cross, understand violation, particularly as You carried the weight of every sexual sin ever committed. Oh Jesus, just as You triumphed over every sin when God the Father raised You to life, please show my friend that morning is coming, resurrection awaits on the horizon. Bring life from death. Beauty from chaos. Hope from despair. Clean from unclean. Heal, restore, and renew. Amen.

# INTRODUCTION

## WHY I WROTE THIS BOOK

*"If the Lord had not been my help, my soul would've lived in the land of silence."*

This book started with my post, "The Sexy Wife I Can't Be" on the blog Deeper Church.[1] In it I wrote about my own struggle with sex in the aftermath of sexual abuse. I figured some people would resonate—that usually happens when I'm gut honest—but I wasn't emotionally prepared for the onslaught of comments and stories. Deeper Church had to switch servers—so much traffic came their way that day.

And the comments. Oh the comments. So many stories shared, some for the very first time. I felt their anguish, carrying their words in my heart. That week my soul heavied. Because how can it be that so much pain in the world has gone unnoticed? Why is it that so many suffer in silence, trying to cope with haunting memories alone? Why haven't we talked about it?

The silence should not be.

Which is why I'm writing this book.

If you're like me, you may feel that the sexual abuse you endured left an indelible mark on your soul, staining your emotional, physical, relational, and sexual health. It has permeated the way you view the world. It scars the way you process information, and it has left you cynical, scared, and hyper-vigilant. I've walked that painful and bewildering path. There have been times when I've yelled (screamed) at God, asking Him why in the world I'd been "entrusted" with this abuse. I've railed at the utter unfairness of it all, suffering for years for other people's sins. Wondering why it is still a struggle for me to enjoy sex. Worrying if I'd ever feel emotionally healthy in sexual abuse's aftermath.

The mark the abuse left has deeply injured me, yet I dare to believe that we serve a God who heals. Not always instantly. It often takes years to lighten a deeply tattooed mark, after all. But He does salve the wounds of sexual abuse. Like Jacob who wrestled with God, we who are sexually abused have our own sparring matches with the Almighty, hurling a slew of why-why-whys and why-why-why-nots His way. Like Jacob, we walk with a limp in the aftermath. Yet, we walk.

I don't have to trod this earth as a marked victim, and neither do you. So I'm writing this book to offer you the hope I have found along the way. To demonstrate the healing possibilities to those of us who have long felt different, dirty. In trying to erase the mark, I've tried many avenues of healing, some successful, some not. I've spent over thirty years of my life pursuing health, and I've gained insight into the healing process. This book represents all the wisdom I've gained—wisdom I want you to have as you chase after the joyful life you hope for.

That doesn't mean your journey will resemble mine. I've never met a human exactly like me (thank goodness!), so my hunch is that we will all heal in us-shaped ways. Often that comes by simply believing that we can heal and having an audacious desire to be whole again. It's my desire that in reading my undecorated story, you will believe healing is possible, and you'll sense God's nearness as you take the next step.

I recently re-read one of my favorite books, *The Rest of God* by Mark Buchanan. One of the chapters addresses healing. He writes about how we can go on in our lives without healing, becoming quite content in our pain. "Restoration meddles with what they've learned to handle, removes what they've learned to live with, bestows what they've learned to live without."[2] In short, we become adept at living with a gaping wound. It's our comfortable place, what we embrace as our lot in life. Dysfunction is our safe place; it's what is knowable and navigable. The prospect of healing frightens us because we don't know what it looks like. Living with freedom would be new, different—alien to the way we've conducted our lives until this moment.

Mind if I ask you a question? Does it frighten you that you might not heal? Do you worry that it's too scary to try? What if you find you can't be healed? Not healing would be devastating, so you might believe you'd be better off not trying at all.

Your fear of healing is likely fueled by Satan, who is aptly called the Father of Lies. Why would he care if you heal or not? Because he knows that if he can keep you shackled to the past, shuddering in the darkness, you'll never understand healthy, beautiful relationships. You'll shrink back from life, people, and opportunity because of your story. Saint Irenaeus purportedly wrote, "The glory of God is man fully alive."[3] When was the last time you felt utterly, joyfully alive? Does that seem impossible to you? Has dysfunction become your comfortable, cozy place? Does growth seem terrifying?

I won't lie to you.

Sometimes healing and growth excruciate. Today I received a tweet that indicated this agony: "But did you ever get to a point where you felt like you couldn't deal with the healing process?" And then: "I just feel like I can't do it anymore, it's so painful!"

Tears, heaving sobs, and a feeling of being lost accompany a healing journey. But you can't have change without tension and fear. Any great adventure has obstacles, right?

## THE HEALING TRAIL

In my book *Thin Places*, I likened the journey of healing to a mountainside tunnel. It goes something like this.

You're hiking along a difficult trail, shrouded by looming, arm-waving evergreens. The air is invigorated with the scent of pine, and in the darkness of the forest you are grateful to be alive. Because at least you can walk. Ahead of you is a tunnel hewn from the rock, created by engineers in the 1920s to simplify a train's route, but now it's for folks like you, hikers discovering the beauty of a mountain. There's a problem, though. It's terribly dark inside. Somehow, you know that if you walk into the darkness, you'll be attacked. So you hesitate. You pace outside the tunnel, wondering if it would be safe to venture inward. You look behind you at how far you've come, how much the forest has sheltered you. There is safety in the path you took, but this tunnel represents mystery.

From inside you hear a voice like the voice of God, a thundering, beckoning, frightening, beautiful voice saying, "I will be with you in the tunnel. Don't be afraid." You debate whether to step inside. You stretch your toe into darkness.[4]

And then, you take the first steps into the tunnel. You freeze. But Jesus takes you by the hand and sits beside you. Although He already knows your story, He asks you to retell it, and while you do, a giant IMAX screen illuminates the tunnel. When the words of your devastation leave your mouth, the story comes alive before you, stunning you to your spot, trembling you inside and out. Technicolor is almost too much to bear. And then you hear weeping.

Is it yours? Could be. But it's mixed together with the weeping of the Almighty who wept at Lazarus's tomb at the finality of death and the grief of life.

Something in you died when that person (or people) stole from you, and you've had a life of grieving your innocence ever since. Jesus laments alongside you in the dark place as the credits roll. He opens up your wounds, not to frighten you, but to fix you. He cleans the festering sore, which hurts like the dickens, then sews it up. It leaves a scar. When He's finished, He opens His embrace, and in doing so, you see His scars too. He hung naked on a cross. He received the nails of hatred and violation. His brow still bears the marks of thorns piercing flesh. He understands. Oh how He understands.

He walks through the tunnel alongside you, His scarred hand in yours. The light that comes from the end of the tunnel stuns you, hushes you. Because of the black darkness behind you, the squinting sunshine is even more brilliant.

On the other side of the tunnel is a blessed, joyful light. But more than that, you realize that while you were in the tunnel you'd been climbing above the tree line. Before, you'd been wandering around in a dark forest and now you stand above it. You see mountains majestic, a sky of cumulus clouds, the sun peek-a-booing through them. You see the trail that you traversed as important and necessary, but this new vista fades the pain a bit. You thank God for the necessity of the tunnel, how it became the avenue from back then to right now.

That's the journey I want to take you on in this book. From darkness to light. From fear to hope. From violation to healing. From victimized to victor. From marked to unmarked. From one who was hurt to one who doles out healing. I couldn't, and wouldn't, make this promise if it weren't true in my own life. Jesus has healed (and continues to heal) me, particularly in the area of sex.

Before we begin the journey, let's look at ways sexual abuse can affect us today. But as you do, be careful you don't minimize what happened to you. Dan Allender wrote in *The Wounded Heart* that any kind of unwanted sexual touch is a violation. In surveys and studies, the reaction to, and healing in the aftermath of that touch is oddly similar whether there's been full penetration or an unwanted hand on a leg. Anything that crosses that line leaves a scar. So, as you read this list, see if any of these problems/issues resonate with you. This isn't an exhaustive inventory, but it may help you see how deeply sexual abuse affects you right now. Many of these (but not all) are things I've experienced.

**In Your Sexual Relationship:**

- You are afraid to have sex. In fact, if sex were suddenly erased from planet earth, you would throw a party.
- You can't have sex—it hurts or it doesn't work right.

- You feel guilty for not being "enough" for your spouse, but have no idea how to sufficiently heal in this area to want sex. It's more duty than joy.
- You are compulsive about sex and take extreme risks in your sexual behavior.
- You view sex as a commodity, not as a loving act between two people.
- You are repulsed by sex. Though you might tolerate it for the sake of your loved one, deep down you feel sickened and having to wrestle so much with trying to "like" sex makes you angry.
- You are drawn to pornography. This causes you to feel even more shame.
- You worry that if you learn to enjoy sex you're somehow validating the abuse you experienced.
- You freeze when a trigger or flashback happens during sex, but you don't speak about it, leaving your spouse confused. You are terrified to speak to your spouse about your triggers and flashbacks.
- If you do have sex, you disconnect from the act in order to tolerate it. You're never "in the moment." Instead you float above yourself.
- Or you fantasize to take you out of the equation. You make up stories so it's not actually you having the sex.
- You become so reliant on the fantasies for your pleasure that you don't know how to enjoy sex without them.

- You grow deep resentment toward your spouse and even toward God because you "have" to have sex.
- You have orgasmic difficulties.
- You have zero desire to have sex.
- You have an insatiable desire for sex.

**In Your Emotional Health:**

- Shame is your constant companion. Shameful feelings are familiar and normal—it's how you process life.
- You have memory blocks where you cannot access large chunks of time. You want to know what happened, but are also afraid to uncover the truth.
- You worry that you brought on the abuse yourself and you shame yourself for not breaking free from the abuse sooner.
- You gravitate toward abusive relationships because that is what is known (safe) and what you feel you deserve.
- You feel dirty.
- You've experienced symptoms of Post Traumatic Stress Disorder (PTSD).[5]
- You have had strong feelings of suicide.
- You battle catastrophic thinking—if one thing bad happens, you automatically leap to believing the entire world is falling apart.
- You deny that your past has any bearing on your present or your future, hurting you and others. That was "back then," you argue. It was so long ago, that it no longer affects you, and you don't

need to think about it. And yet, your behavior shows that no matter how long ago it happened, it is having a profound effect on you today.

- You minimize what happened, rationalizing that other people have worse stories, so why should you be affected by your sexual abuse?
- You fear that if you deal with the abuse from the past, you will explode or die or start crying and never stop. You worry you'll become so overcome you might take your life.

## In Your Relationships:

- You feel used easily. If your spouse doesn't pay attention to you during the day and expects to have sex at night, you feel like a prostitute or a gigolo.
- You absolutely need the approval of others to feel okay.
- The word "trust" freaks you out.
- You avoid others because you think you have nothing to offer them.
- You have a titanic fear of being abandoned. That fear controls you, keeps you up at night, and dictates how you act around others.
- You don't know how to process your pain without yelling or acting fearfully inappropriate, so you believe it's better to keep your mouth shut.
- You're good at stuffing your feelings and emotions way down deep.

- You worry that if you talk about the sexual abuse, your family of origin will abandon you (particularly when the abuse happened within the family). You believe telling the truth means you aren't honoring your parents or that you're breaking an unwritten code of silence.
- You harbor deep resentment toward a parent or caretaker who didn't protect you. Sometimes the rage is palpable.
- You have a hard time developing close, intimate relationships.
- To feel safe, you control people and things.
- You have victimized others.
- You have a fear of one gender (either all men or all women).

**In Your Daily Life:**

- You battle an addiction. That addiction fills a hole you can't seem to fill otherwise. Often this addiction is secret.
- You feel you've been marked for sexual abuse, even as an adult. Predators seem to find you.
- You startle easily.
- You are afraid to be alone, particularly at night.
- You have flashbacks and/or nightmares about the abuse.
- You fear being grabbed from behind.
- You are either an obsessive risk taker, or a complete risk-avoider.

- You have carried the secret for years and never let it out because you fear you won't be believed. You wonder if you'll carry it to the grave.
- You walk through life hyper-vigilant, always worried something bad is going to happen.

## In Your Identity:

- You believe you are worthless. In fact, you know you are. Why else would those perpetrators do that to you?
- You overachieve to prove your worth. It has become another form of addiction.
- You underachieve because it's better to remain invisible. And you underachieve because, honestly, why bother succeeding if you're worthless?
- You rebel to gain attention, the crazier the act, the better—anything so someone will pay attention to you.
- You believe you are different from others—and not in a good way.
- You feel you don't belong.
- You feel utterly alone, like no one else in the history of the world understands what it is like to be you.
- You constantly wonder why you are on this earth, other than to be abused and taken advantage of.
- You feel small.
- You often battle insecurity.
- Even when you're complimented, you don't believe the sentiment.

**In Your Health:**

- You deal with panic attacks, sleeplessness, or autoimmune disorders.
- You struggle with a food addiction.
- You're overweight. Your weight keeps you safe from predators, so the thought of losing weight scares you.
- You have a poor body image. Nothing about you is ever perfect or beautiful or handsome or enough.
- You think you will die young.
- You battle depression.
- You fear doctor exams (gynecological or otherwise).
- You battle self-mutilation, anorexia, bulimia, or any self-destructive behavior.

Go back through and circle your struggles, and feel free to add more in the margins. If you're extra daring, share your circles with your closest friend, a counselor, or your spouse. Chances are, folks have no idea how much you've been affected by the past. When I started sharing some of these things with my husband, Patrick, he was surprised and saddened. He had no idea how much grief and shame and sorrow and fear I housed inside myself. It felt therapeutic to share it, but it took me a long time to be brave enough and trust my husband enough to let him know how I felt.[6]

Honestly, I wish I could wave a magic wand and erase the mark from both me and you. I've felt like the writer of Proverbs, "I am weary, O God. I am weary and worn out" (Proverbs 30:1, ESV). But immediate healing doesn't always work—though I would welcome that. Dismantling lies we've lived with for so long takes a lot of time, a lot of truth, and a lot of unconditional love.

The aftermath of sexual abuse is sad and grim, but I thank God that He didn't leave us resourceless. I thank Him that although there is a large swath of devastation, there is also a larger story of reconciliation and redemption. The mark we carry does not need to become our identity. I believe this verse for you: "Surely there is a future, and your hope will not be cut off" (Proverbs 23:18, ESV). I fully believe Jesus can fade the mark, eventually erasing it. He can heal us so much so that we become agents of healing in a sex-injured world.

Still, healing has to be wanted. You can't expect healing to happen magically to you, slipped under your pillow by the Healing Fairy. It has to be pursued. You cannot and will not heal in passivity. When Jesus asked the man at the pool of Bethesda if he wanted to get well, the man never answered him. He had been sitting by that pool for over three decades, waiting passively for something to happen. The beauty of that story is that even though the man had no response, Jesus graced him with outrageous healing.

So even if you start this book with no desire to heal, mad at the world and bitter toward others, with no unction to get better, it's my prayer that Jesus would woo you toward the wanting of it all. Like Peter whose faith faltered as he stepped onto the water, Jesus didn't let him sink into the waters because of his frailty, He lifted him from the murky depths.

My story is simply this: "He lifted me out of the pit of despair, out of the mud and the mire. He set my feet on solid ground and steadied me as I walked along" (Psalm 40:2, NLT). That is my deepest, utmost prayer for you as you read this book.

# PART ONE

# STORIES

In order to understand my own healing story, I need to share where I came from, what I endured, and how my marriage intersected it. If you're sensitive to sexual abuse references, note that Chapter One is where I share my own rape story. Though not in detail by any stretch, it may trigger flashbacks.

# CHAPTER
# 1

# MY STORY

## WHAT HAPPENED WHEN I WAS FIVE YEARS OLD

*"For dogs encompass me; a company of evildoers encircles me."*

PSALM 22: 16, ESV

## WARNING: TRIGGER ALERT

This book didn't just begin with a viral blog post. It birthed years and years ago beneath the evergreen trees of my childhood, a story I'm no longer afraid to tell straight. It's a tale I kept silent for a decade, unable to articulate the violation. I believe it even started before my kindergarten year in the cacophony of free sex and readily available drugs that typified my childhood.

God knit me in my mother's womb when she was still a teenager. My father had seduced her, he a university teacher's assistant studying for his PhD in English, she a student. They did the noble thing and married.

I don't know if my mother knew my father's sexual addiction when they married, and I'm still not entirely sure what happened during those few years of marriage. I do know he scared her. He cajoled her to pose for unbecoming pictures—something she refused. It didn't take long for her to divorce him. At this point, my memory, which was sharp as a tack until then, blurs. I actually do remember a snippet of toddlerhood vividly, but then blankness. I've asked every family member what happened next in my life, but none will talk. Once I directly asked a relative, "What happened to me between the ages of two to five?"

"Why dig up the past?" she said, then promptly changed the subject.

I've heard one possible rumor that I lived with my mom, moving constantly to unsafe places. I can't substantiate it or remember if it is true. But if it is the truth, the puzzle of my life starts to make sense. For I have this desire for home, a huge fear (like panic) of not having food, and when rape knocked on my door in my fifth year, I seemed to walk into it easily, as if I'd resigned myself to its inevitability. I have a sneaking suspicion that I'd been molested prior to my memories of the year of rapes. But this is just conjecture.

I can prove none of my hunches. Which, for this investigative reporter type, drives me batty. But perhaps God shields us from the whole truth of our lives until we can handle it. And if we can't, Heaven will heal even our unseen wounds.

Two of the most problematic things I've dealt with in this journey toward sexual healing involves forgiving my parents for two infractions. One: if my mom married a sexually disturbed man who made her afraid, why did she still send me to him every other weekend after the divorce? The only thing I can piece together is something I've dealt with all my life—this feeling that I wasn't wanted, that I was a terrible mistake and inconvenience. (I own this, understanding it may not be the truth, though I *felt* it was.) So she seemed to let her desire for freedom override her fears for me. Away I went. The other: when I was five and the older boys raped me, I know my behavior changed, and there most likely was evidence. Neither she, my stepfather or my father didn't seem to notice. I still have a hard time reconciling their lack of attentiveness. Honestly, that anger has been the hardest to process. And yet, I'm learning grace. As a parent, I make hundreds of mistakes. Lately God has given me a heart of compassion for my parents, something that took years and years to come by.

Maybe you understand? Have you experienced greater anger toward the person who didn't protect you?

I know my story is not nearly as awful as many others. I've had the privilege (and sadness) of hearing hundreds of stories, so I know mine may seem small. To others, it may seem far more devastating than their own. The degree of the sexual abuse is not the point. I've learned that with sexual violation to compare your story with another is only a useless diversion and not helpful to bring healing. One friend felt her wounds were small in comparison to another woman's horrific story. But the woman with the "harder" story said, "You may have had your leg (figuratively) cut off at the calf, and mine may be cut off at the thigh, but neither one of us can walk."

Thus I tell my story, not to glory in the details and trigger your own flashbacks, but so you know I understand violation, and I have deep, deep empathy for you.

## MY STORY

When I was five years old, I attended kindergarten. Although most people I know remember their kindergarten teacher, I don't. I remember every single teacher I've had since then, but I can't conjure up my kindergarten teacher's name, and certainly not her face. When she alerted my parents to my inability to do well in the oddly-named subject Cooperation, she did not know the nightmares I faced at my babysitter's home.

Babysitter Eva loomed large in my life, a chain-smoking woman who took in kids to pay the rent. She didn't really like children in my estimation, and in her care I knew once again I was in the way. So much so that when two teenage brothers asked if they could take me off her hands, she agreed quickly, shooing me out the door. As far as I remember, they did no grooming, no easing me into what would happen next. They took me to a deep ravine near my elementary school and said something to the effect of, "Do you want to have babies someday?"

Me, who wanted to nurture anything, including my posse of thrift store stuffed animals, nodded. But I knew something wasn't right. The look in their eyes, the leer beneath the glint, the crazy frenzy with which they worked to pull down my pants—all these added up to panic. I remember saying no. I remember struggling, but they were too strong for me. I remember the burning, the fire inside me never extinguishing. I remember the grass and rocks they placed within me, how I had to pull them out later, ashamed, trembling, bleeding.

Every day they came for me at Eva's in the late afternoon. They violated little me in countless ways in different venues. They told me, "If you tell your parents, we will kill them." I believed them. So I kept my mouth shut.

In the ravines, I kept my focus on the evergreen trees that had often seen me naked from the waist down, shaking, and silently crying. They'd become my friends in a way. They'd given me something to escape to, a place where nature reigned, the sun shined beyond, and life could be tolerated. I flew there while the boys took turns. Some kids who experience violation in such a way do the same thing, but they splinter into different personalities. Me, I watched the tree limbs sway. I invented an imaginary best friend. I learned not to cry.

I distinctly remember the boy's violation of me in their bunk-bedded room, their mother singing in the kitchen making cookies. She offered me some after they'd torn me apart. What did she think her sons were doing with a five-year-old girl? Even now as I write this, I get fiery mad at her, at Eva, at my teacher. Why did no one connect the dots? Or did they not want to face the dots? Was it too terrible to think about? Or just too inconvenient?

I needed a hero, but none swooped from the sky, Ironman-like, to rescue me. I wondered why in the world was I on this earth. I was a mistake to be violated at will, unworthy of protection.

One grace God gave me during this time: I knew what those boys did was wrong. They were bad. That I didn't deserve what they did. I realize now this kind of thinking is rare. So many sexual abuse victims blame themselves, think they've enticed somehow.

Eventually those brothers—who wore Boy Scout uniforms—invited their friends to join in the "fun." I became their free entertainment most afternoons. Something rose up in me, a holy roar perhaps? I somehow knew that if I continued down this path, I would be destroyed. So eventually I decided to tell Eva what happened. It took me months to conjure up the gumption because the only word the perpetrators used to describe what they did was the dreaded F word, and I knew that if I whispered that word, I'd get Ivory soap thrust in my mouth. I finally overcame that fear, decided that a soapy mouth would be better than what those boys did to me. I also feared for my parents' lives, wondering if me telling Eva the F word counted toward their death sentence. Would those boys know where my real father lived? Would they hunt him down? Would they kill my mother? My stepfather?

I swallowed fear one afternoon after the boys returned me and asked Eva to please come near. I remember how tall she loomed, how her head seemed near the ceiling. I have a clear memory of asking her to bend down to me. I cupped my hands over her ears and whispered, "Those boys f---ed me." I remember the snap of her neck, the way she loomed again, the look on her face.

Then she uttered the five words that would ruin my life: "I will tell your mother."

I believed her.

I went home that night, practically elated. Those boys and their lust-crazy friends wouldn't be allowed to take me to ravines, the evergreen trees waving their hands above me.

The next day, I'm sure I wore a smile when I arrived at Eva's house. I half expected her to nurture me, to feel sorry for me, to protect me now that she knew about the F word. I imagined her telling my mom in hushed tones, my mom's eyes widening, then turning to tears. I pictured her speaking with my stepfather, a man I feared, telling him about the horrible thing that happened to me, that horrible word reverberating between them. But I was too young to understand the ways of adults, though the boys' rape had inaugurated me into their world far too soon. I was too naive to realize that babysitters who let older boys take little girls probably already knew what they were doing to me. Or that if she told as she said she would, she could be arrested, along with those boys, for allowing such a thing. Her "childcare" operation would be shut down and the rent wouldn't be paid.

So I believed she told. And I believed my mom would rescue me. I hadn't made the connection yet that my mom took me back to Eva the chain smoking babysitter. Had I been more mature or logical, I would've realized this didn't make sense.

The rapid knock at Eva's back door chilled me. They were there. Again.

I heard her say, "Oh sure, she's here. Let me get her."

And off I went to the woods, to the tree limbs, to the burning that never went away.

At this point I crumpled inside. Eva wouldn't protect me. How evil was she? I still can't comprehend it. Sometimes I imagine what it would be like to punch her, to see the blood drain from her nose. But more than Eva, my mother didn't protect me. I (wrongly) believed she knew, but didn't care enough to rescue me.

## ANOTHER LAYER OF HEALING

Years and years later after I'd written about this story in my memoir, *Thin Places*, I experienced cathartic healing involving that terrible F word. I sat in a recording studio reading the audio book, shocking the poor guys behind the wall of glass. When we neared the part where I was supposed to say the forbidden word, he said, "Mary, you can say any word that starts with F. I don't care what you use. We'll end up bleeping it out." Since I couldn't remember saying that word out loud, I figured I'd say a *Battlestar Gallactica* "frak" and be done with it.

But when the sentence loomed and I saw the f--- staring at me on the page, I realized in a flash of aha that the word was ugly. It did connote exactly what those boys did to me. I read that sentence, expletive and all. And healing rushed in. It felt good to say the awful word so stark like that. In saying it raw and real, I was finally able to holler the badness, to assign a word to the violation. The producer's eyes widened when I swore, then he smiled and gave me a thumbs up. I think he knew I'd just experienced catharsis, another sentence written in my healing story.

## HOW I ENDURED

At five years old, I knew this truth about the world: not one human being would inconvenience themselves to take care of me. Only I could. So I did. After the boys took their turns again the day after I told Eva, I decided the next day would be different.

After half-day kindergarten I ate lunch, then took a Rip Van Winkle nap. I slept through two o'clock, three, four, five. The knock came, but Eva, who obviously didn't want to be bothered, told the boys to go away. She couldn't be inconvenienced to wake me up. Thank God.

My plan worked so well, every afternoon at Eva's became one long nap.

As my kindergarten chapter ended, my mother and stepfather decided their hippy marriage, bound together by parties, should end. This meant we'd move away, far, far away from the boys, the tree limbs, and the chain-smoking babysitter.

## THE MARK

After telling Eva and getting no response, I didn't utter a peep about the sexual abuse for ten years. It became the secret I kept locked way back inside myself. That didn't mean I stuffed the memories. They still woke me up at night. I'd have nightmares of the boys, of chases, of murderers cornering me. In daytime, I'd fantasize about being Cindy Brady of *The Brady Bunch* belonging to the perfect family, riding in a wood-siding clad station wagon. The problem with my secret, though, was the merit badge the Boy Scout brothers etched into me—a "please come abuse me" mark that lived like a lighthouse beacon on my forehead for every possible predator to see.

And see it, they did. It seemed every time I turned around, a predator found me. In my barn, a hired worker came way too near, touching my shoulder, telling me I was pretty while I stood alone in horse-manure caked boots. I ran. In a treehouse a boy grabbed the waistband of his Toughskin jeans and yanked them earthward— told me in no uncertain terms that we were playing doctor. I ran. An older brother of some kids I babysat touched my shoulders and eased his way down. I ran. A boyfriend tried the same dance. I ran. And even into adulthood, I've realized the mark remains. I've encountered predatory men who seem to know I'm a target. I've had to learn the art and grit of creating obvious boundaries to protect myself.

My father contributed to the mark. His is a story still very hard for me to make sense of, let alone tell. But he crossed many parent/child boundaries with me. He had me bathe him in a claw-foot bathtub, a full-length mirror to the right of him. I had to take the soap and run it all over his body. He hosted naked people in his house, something I thought normal until much, much later when I realized not everyone's fathers had nude people roaming the halls. He took pictures of unclothed women—their bodies in death-like positions—then showed them to me, seemingly wanting my approval for his "art." He took pictures of me sans clothes next to another naked girl. She looked frightened. Unfortunately, I looked comfortable. This kind of activity had become terribly normalized for me.

This all ended the day my father died. I was ten years old. I believed he was a hero. I hadn't realized how warped he'd been. Because he seemed to love me and like to be around me, I felt his loss in my gut, my soul, my world. Still not close to my mom, but connected to my second stepfather, I mourned, hero-less.

## MORE SHAME

The sexually charged atmosphere in which I grew up, coupled with what those boys did to me, warped my view of sex. I was both scandalized and enticed by it. I found pornography in my home—and I consumed it. I felt guilty indulging in it, but also alive. I wrestled with this addiction (yes, as a girl) for several years post-redemption. Sex, as a result, became dirty, terrible, and only relegated to aberration.

Although determined to be pure, to choose virginity for marriage, I still felt defiled not only by what those boys did to me, but also because of my own addiction, following in my father's footsteps. I wanted to be a girl Jesus would be proud of, but I carried this dark, dark secret. I told no one for many years, and only found freedom when I shared my struggle with a trusted friend. I learned then that Satan loves to keep us held hostage in our minds, making us believe we're scum, that we're the only one dealing with these addictions, that we're unredeemable. What he knows is that if we dare let our secrets out into the light, we will be set free. And I was. Not instantly. But that's when the healing in that part of my life began.

Once I reached adolescence, because I wanted a father's love, I had this terrible need to be noticed by boys. Before I met Jesus, during my suicide-contemplation years when my mom's third marriage deteriorated, I wanted a boy to ask me out, love me, give me a long hug, and tell me everything would be okay. Problem was, every time I liked a boy I would panic the moment he'd return the favor. My first kiss came in the sixth grade, sloppy and creepy in our town's only movie theater. It so freaked me out that I broke up with him. The same thing happened in the eighth grade, then the tenth grade. I wanted to be loved, but the moment any affection came my way, I ran.

## ENTER JESUS

I met Jesus when I was fifteen and nearly at the end of myself. I heard all about Him at Young Life. During my sophomore year, in the fall, I attended a weekend camp where I heard the whole raucous gospel, of Jesus stooping to this pain-stained world, wearing earth's shoes, and walking around thirty-three years. He loved the outcasts (and oh how I knew I was one). He dignified the broken. He loved the unwanted. The more I heard His stories, the more I fell in love with Him. When I learned of His death on my behalf (someone would die for me?), I cried. I remembered my own father in the grave, the finality of death. But Jesus resurrected Himself, defying the specter Death, and wooing me toward a new, new life.

I surrendered to Jesus under an evergreen tree, its hands waving high, high above me. I still consider the irony. The place of my deepest violation became my trysting place of redemption. Set free. Loved. Wanted. Sacrificed for. "Oh the deep, deep love of Jesus, vast unmeasured, boundless free. Flowing as a mighty ocean over me. Underneath me, all around me is the current of His love."[7]

When I met Jesus, I started telling my story. The sexual abuse came out, first to my mom who initially didn't believe me. I had to re-tell the story before she understood. Then I told the story to my Young Life leaders who must've been shocked. For a long period of time I became an over-sharer, telling everyone what I went through. I did it to get attention, to say, "Hey, look at what I went through, and I'm okay." I naively believed that 2 Corinthians 5:17 ("Therefore, if anyone is in Christ, the new creation has come: The old has gone, the new is here!" ESV) meant that I'd experience complete healing now that I knew Jesus. I thought that as a new Christian, I would be instantly healed from every memory, every hurt, every pain, and henceforth would be stable, happy, whole, and fine forever and ever amen.

## THE STRUGGLE

But that past, that great big past, haunted me. It followed me to college where I summarily fell apart over and over again. Still afraid of men, yet needy of them, I continued to woo them, then push them away. I wanted to be whole, but I didn't know how to be. I'll share more about this time in my life later because it was the seedbed of most of my healing, but suffice to say, God met me there through the power of community and prayer. After four years of healing prayers by friends and my church, I believed I'd been healed. Fully. Completely. Never to be revisited.

I've since realized that I had a faulty view of healing. It doesn't just happen once for all, particularly when it comes to sexual abuse. Healing is layers. Healing is time. Healing is excruciating. Once you think it's done, it's not. Triggers continue. And when they do, I ask myself, *Didn't God heal me in college? Why am I revisiting this?* I chastise myself for being weak. I wonder if the healing I'd experienced faded and why.

When I met my husband, something felt different. Prior to him, I'd had one relationship in college that I thought was love, only to be dumped (thank God in retrospect!). God used that dismissing to show me how hungry I had become for a man to fill my heart. I realized how dangerous my need was, and I limped toward making Jesus my everything. With Patrick, for the very first time, I had peace. I didn't need him to fill the gaping Daddy wound, and besides that, Patrick made me laugh like crazy. A breath of beautifully fresh air, he was. We talked about everything, sharing our stories, our pasts, our love for Jesus, our penchant for missions. We dated six months, then were engaged. I knew. I just knew. He was (and is) God's best for me.

I did tell him about the sexual abuse. I did tell him I'd be frightened on our wedding night. But neither of us knew how hard it would be.

## FROM PATRICK:

(Note: Throughout the book, my husband, Patrick, will offer his side of things in hopes of helping spouses or friends of abuse victims. They, too, struggle with the abuse, and healing for them is also a difficult process.)

> One of the gifts I gave to Mary was making sure she felt safe and cared for. Not only her, but when we had children I made sure that they would be safe, no matter the circumstance. In reality, I don't have that much control. We had to have babysitters. We let our kids stay over at friends' houses. There were times that we wondered if they were truly safe when they were out of our sight, though we tried to know as much as we could about our children's friends and their families. I thank God that He has protected them. But I think that my concern for their safety was something that Mary never felt she had growing up. Knowing and

seeing that I wasn't a casual father and husband was something she treasured.

I also get very angry about what these boys did to Mary. I wish I had been there to protect her when it happened, to be a hero standing in front of her daring them to get through me to get to her.

Even though I know that the majority of abusers have been abused themselves, I don't really feel any empathy for what these boys did. I look forward to the day when justice is served—perhaps it already has. What they did is not fair or right or justified. They created a wound in my wife that I also have suffered from and I wouldn't wish on anyone.

I am thankful that as Mary grew up God did protect her from the effects of her abuse. She did not get into drugs. She was not promiscuous or rebellious. But that doesn't mean she was whole when I met her. She had deep wounds, deeper than even I was aware. She was on the path to healing, which, if we had met sooner in life probably would have scared me off. As she said above, the path to healing is one of endurance and peeling back layer by layer. I am thankful that God saw fit to allow me to walk that path with her, because it has caused me to be a conduit of that healing.

# CHAPTER
# 2

# PATRICK AND ME

## HOW SEXUAL ABUSE AFFECTED OUR MARRIAGE

*Three things are too wonderful for me;*
*four I do not understand:*
*the way of an eagle in the sky,*
*the way of a serpent on a rock,*
*the way of a ship on the high seas,*
*and the way of a man with a virgin.*

PROVERBS 30:18–19, ESV

On our wedding night, I cried.

Oddly, not because sex loomed, but because I missed my father.

He hadn't been there for so many milestones, and now he'd missed another. In retrospect, I've made a tentative peace with his death. I now see it as God's protection of me. I do believe my dad was subtly (and not so subtly) grooming me for abuse. His penchant for younger, and younger women had become apparent. I could have been his next victim.

I remember sitting on the corner of the bed on our wedding night, shivering. We'd been married during a rare cold snap in Seattle. The bed and breakfast Patrick had reserved called the night before the wedding and cancelled—no electricity. We now sat in a smoking room of a local hotel, two double beds. Patrick tried to build a fire, but it had been so cold, the air had forced wood smoke into our room, causing the alarm to go off. Men knocked at the door with extinguishers and a ladder, while I sat in my going away dress.

## FEAR

As I look back on that night now, I wish we would've waited. I was just too scared, too damaged, too worried to really engage in the act of marriage. But I also have this I-want-to-please-everyone mentality, so I wanted to be the good Proverbs 31 wife who did what was supposed to be done on her wedding night. Patrick didn't know just how petrified I was. Had he known, I think he would've seen the wisdom in a delay so we could become comfortable with each other, and I could deal with the fear. Instead, I stuffed it. And tried to slip into my new role as wife as I slipped on lingerie.

To add to my angst, when the gynecologist performed his exam a few weeks prior to the wedding night, he traumatized me. As I crawled northward on the cold metal table, he told me I'd have a very hard time on my wedding night, then promptly wrote me a prescription for "something to take the edge off." I didn't fill the script, but I did nurse even more anxiety.

Needless to say, it wasn't romantic movie sex. My closest friend saw me the next day. "Well?" she said. "How was it?" As if it were a competition I'd tackled for the first time, like running my first half marathon.

Do I rate it? Tell the truth? Honestly, I was glad it was over, but the sting I felt reminded me of the pain in the woods with those boys. I prayed it would get better. "It was great," I said.

We honeymooned in Mexico, getting used to each other, me still trying to adjust to my role as the sexy wife. I found myself disconnecting even then, reverting back to the time in the woods when I'd watch the tree limbs far above. If I disconnected, I could tolerate the act.

Another thing felt even scarier, though. When I truly felt alive and joyful in the act of marriage, I had this sinking feeling. If I liked sex, I was, in a strange way, legitimizing the abuse. Enjoying it now meant I had enjoyed it back then. I now know that what I felt was warped, but it's been my battle ever since. If I dare "give in" to sexual bliss, I feel dirty, perverted. Enjoying sex danced me closer to the line of becoming more like my father, one of my greatest fears I've dealt with in the sexual arena.

Looking back, it's even more ironic that I cried about my father on my wedding night, because the specter of him haunted the marriage bed. He was most likely a sex addict, a creator of pornography, one who preyed on women.

Can you see how that might terrify me? If I fully enjoyed sex then I would summarily be saying what those boys did was okay. And I'd be inching closer to becoming an addict of perversion like my father. Sex was a scary, untamed animal I dared not coddle. So I performed, but I kept my heart far, far away.

Of course this was unfair to my husband. He didn't do those awful things to me. He wasn't addicted to porn or sex or exploitation as my father had been. But he has had to suffer through my disconnection for many years. There have been times I've tried to reconnect to the act, and I know he appreciates that, but in doing so, I start panicking again. I can say that over the years I've gradually gotten better at engaging, but the healing has certainly not been sudden, but the slowest kind of gradual that you can imagine. Snail healing, really.

## NOT ENOUGH SEX

Besides my own issues, I constantly worried that I wasn't having enough sex with my husband. I fretted a lot about this, and to be honest, I still do. Since I'm a pleaser at heart, I have this belief that men turn blue if they don't have enough sex. This, of course, is a low view of men, most likely imprinted on me from my father's addiction. Nonetheless, I have suffered hours, days, months of anxiety about this. No matter how much I give in, I don't feel it's enough.

This was much worse when we were first married, and my husband's appetites were stronger. I felt guilty if he'd gone several days without sex, but I never thought to acknowledge my own indifference to it. There were times, particularly when Patrick was emotionally distant from me, that having sex felt like prostitution to me. I was paying a debt, so to speak, to someone who hadn't known me as a person. Eventually (it took years), I shared this with Patrick, that I feel used very easily, and that for me to engage in the act of marriage, I needed to know I was a person first, that I was valuable enough to share thoughts and feelings with. Otherwise, I'd do the act begrudgingly because I was supposed to.

## COMMUNICATING ABOUT SEX

Talking about sex has been excruciating as well. The first few times Patrick had to bring it up, I responded with a red face, a pit in my stomach. I ran from the room. I didn't want to talk about it. Sex was an act to be performed with the lights off, no chatting, certainly without a commentary about it either before or after.

I didn't want to tell him what I liked. I didn't want to share what bothered me. But eventually, I had to, because some of what he did (though he didn't know it) triggered me back to the woods with those boys. It was a supreme act of sheer grit that I was finally able to communicate to Patrick about what freaked me out, what made my blood run cold, what turned me completely off.

It's a testament of twenty-three years of long-suffering marriage that we can talk about sex now without me freaking out or turning crimson or running from the room. It's not easy. I still struggle, but sharing has become easier. In order to have this sort of conversation, there has to be mutual understanding and affection for each other. There has to be a commitment to love despite hearing things you might not want to hear. There has to be a willingness on both sides to work through sexual issues.

## WE ALL HAVE ISSUES

Truly, the most healing part of our adventure together came when Patrick began to look at his own issues. I'd always been the needy one, the broken one, the one with the sordid, painful past. It became our dance to address all of Mary's problems. Which was fine, except that Patrick had issues from the past that needed to be dealt with too. When he began to open up about his own struggles, whether it be about sex or intimacy or fears or vulnerable places in his heart, I no longer felt like Poor Broken Mary who always needing fixing. Camaraderie returned to our marriage in light of Patrick daring to address his own healing.

## THE SEXY WIFE CONFERENCE

Over a decade of guilt into the marriage, I attended a conference to help me become what I perceived my husband wanted me to become. It was a sexy wife conference, where the speakers talked about being sexually available to our spouses. We should write on our calendars reminders to think about sex all day long so we'd be ready. We should be willing to let our husbands eat strawberries off our bellies. We should embrace adventure and whimsy, maybe even role-playing. We should shed that old coat of "sex being naughty" and embrace our hot, sexy selves. This is not easy to do in an evangelical culture that demonizes sex before marriage, then calls it awesome the moment you say, "I do."

It's hard to make that gigantic leap from forbidden to fantastic.

I shrunk inside myself at that conference. Felt guilt-ier. Yet another set of rules I wouldn't be able to live up to in the marriage bed arena. I took notes, but wondered if I could ever overcome my fears to do even one thing on the list. Honestly, what they shared sounded shameful, and I knew I'd feel more and more like a prostitute if I implemented their suggestions.

These women had good things in mind. They understood that husbands were discontented, and they offered practical solutions. They'd quoted scripture, particularly the juicy passages from the Bible's Sex Manual: The Song of Solomon—the book of the Bible that is now seen as prescriptive for married life. The speakers inferred that if married couples are truly committed to marital fidelity, we'll constantly be living in this state of perpetual wedded, sexual bliss.

## SOLOMON A MARITAL ROLE MODEL?

If perpetual bliss is the standard, if we are always wowed and awed by our spouses, when is there a need for forgiveness, acceptance, forbearance, love, kindness, selflessness? The real beauty of marriage is that two flawed people living under one roof are choosing to be faithful to each other.

I believe strongly that some of these Song of Solomon studies set up a false picture of the reality of marriage because marriages have seasons—both in and out of bed. Sometimes passionate, sometimes exhausted. Sometimes married love is plain old comfortable. Sometimes it's ho-hum, and sometimes Oh, Wow! But to think the Oh, Wow! should be normative in marriage places extra pressure on couples to attain an impossible ideal. No couple should feel as though they are "missing out" if they genuinely love each other, are satisfied with each other, and are genuinely happy, just because they're not wildly passionate 365, 24/7.

Although passion is biblical, the idea that every sexual encounter should be the perfect, passionate 10 is not.

Honestly, I will never measure up to that pesky Shulamite woman in the Song of Solomon. And in some cases, by acting like her, I violate my own conscience.

Because I love my husband, I take care of myself. He takes care of himself because he loves me. I disappoint him. He disappoints me. But we are faithful nonetheless. We are walking together, discovering the love of Jesus within each of us, sacrificing for the other, being an example of humility and authenticity to our children, and loving each other despite our shortcomings. That's my picture of marital love. Isn't that how Jesus treats us, His church? With grace? With kindness? With beauty? With hope?

But all that beauty and hope dissipated in that conference, particularly when I realized the speakers were speaking to a room where, if stats play out correctly, 40 % of the women had been sexually assaulted. How would they handle this sexy wife paradigm?

In the midst of all the rhetoric, I stopped feeling anxious about my own shortcomings and starting having an empathy attack for all the other women in the room who shrunk inside themselves like I had. Where were the women who stood up for them? What sort of secret shame did victims nurse? What about those who flashed back every single time they had sex? How would the Song of Solomon been written had his lover had a sexually abusive past?

Probably a lot more running away, than being caught.

## JUST GET OVER IT

I returned from that conference, oddly, determined to be better. Even though it made me angry, their words needled their way onto my "should" list. I tried their techniques for a month, to a much happier husband, but I couldn't sustain them, which then left me feeling guiltier.

I learned we can decorate the outsides of ourselves as much as we can. We can create sexual to-do lists and choose to think about sex all day, but if our heart isn't changed, it won't sustain, and we'll be left feeling even worse about ourselves.

## AND YET . . .

The last few years of our marriage I've noticed a subtle shift in my husband. I hope it's not a giving up, a throwing up of his hands about our frequency or lack thereof. I hope it's something God has wrought in him, a holy patience, a joyful thankfulness when sex does occur, and a much-needed lack of pressure. It endears me to him, this new attitude. And when I feel bad that I haven't performed enough, he is quick to hug me, offer me grace, and assure me of his love. This has taken a long time, but it's a good place. A healing place.

## FROM PATRICK:

Expectations. When I don't get them met, it puts me in a pretty foul mood. If I don't get the raise I'm expecting, if I call a meeting and everyone is late, if the service or food I get at a restaurant aren't up to snuff, I get a little angry. Sometimes a lot angry. This is an area in my life I struggle with daily. I have high expectations of people and when they don't meet them, I put up a wall of judgment. Not a good character trait, I know. But I am sure I am not alone.

So getting married was no different. I had expectations of Mary that, frankly, we had not talked about before marriage. I am not sure how that conversation would have gone anyway. All I knew is that once we were married, everything was legal. I had no problem turning the evangelical switch that sex is naughty before marriage, but everything goes afterward. My expectation was that she would feel that same way. The problem was she did not seem that into it. It felt like she was having sex out of duty not out of desire. As a result, I felt unloved.

You don't get married to feel unloved, and I had a difficult time understanding why she felt this way. I thought eventually the Christian guilt would subside, but it didn't. I tried to connect with her in other ways. I remember giving her a word picture about what it felt like for me. I told her it was like I was in a swimming pool enjoying the water and she was on top of a diving platform too afraid to jump in. Even though she could see it was fine in the pool, it felt like she was unwilling to engage. This helped her see my struggle, and to gain a little more trust.

But I also had to work on my own expectations of her, and the anger I held onto when she didn't meet them. God has worked miracles in my life in this area. One thing He brought me back to Ephesians 5:25. "Husbands, love your wives, as Christ loved the church and gave himself up for her" (ESV). This is a heavy, heavy imperative. The church, I am sure, often fails to meet Christ's expectation for his Body. But what does He do? He loves her. And I need to be in a place in my relationship with Him where I can demonstrate understanding and grace the way He does, not holding on to anger and grudges and resentment.

PART TWO

# YOUR HEALING STORY

There is hope! You do have a healing story, even if you're daring to take the very first step by reading *Not Marked*. The following chapters highlight pathways I've found essential in the healing journey—traits like guts, grace, prayer and forgiveness.

# CHAPTER
# 3

# CULTIVATE COURAGE

## HOW TELLING YOUR STORY LEADS TO FREEDOM

*"Whoever isolates himself seeks his own desire;*

*he breaks out against all sound judgment."*

PROVERBS 18:1, ESV

Right after my memoir, *Thin Places*, released, I launched a website called *My Family Secrets*. My thought behind it was that folks needed an anonymous place to share their family secrets—those malevolent things that kept people up at night, but never see the light of day. I figured if I could provide a platform, abuse victims would share.

They did.

Such awful, painful, excruciating stories. Although I firmly believe a story is best shared in the context of community, I know that catharsis might first have to come tentatively, shared anonymously like that. Eventually I took the site down, not because it wasn't helping folks get free from the darkness of their stories, but because me, being an empathetic person down to my core, couldn't handle it anymore. Too many stories without faces, touch, or connection just left me feeling like this world is a terrible place with terrible people doing terrible things.

If you've never told your story to any other person, writing it down first to share with no one would be a good first step. But ultimately that first step is the beginning of a journey of letting others come into your story, love you through it, weep alongside you, and pray you toward healing.

## HEALING COMES FROM STORYTELLING

Here's the gut-honest truth: I would not be okay if I had not told my story. I wouldn't be writing this book. I most likely would be divorced, broken, possibly institutionalized, most likely suicidal.

Why? Because an untold story never heals.

It just festers inside and hurts the people you love most because you can't help but act differently when that story is contained inside you. It materializes in your actions, attitudes, and the fearful way you live your life. It's like trying to submerge a basketball in a swimming pool. You can do it for a period of time, but you cannot sustain it. Eventually the ball surfaces, usually by hurtling into the air with dramatic flourish.

Let me ask you this: Are you bone tired? Do you feel like your life is a constant struggle to keep your story contained? Do you secretly feel that you're different from everyone else on this planet because of your untold story? Do you have flashbacks? Triggers? A high amount of irrational fears? Does the landscape of your mind look chaotic and frenzied?

I'm not a psychologist by any stretch (with my empathy bent, I'd go nutty), but I can say that finding a safe place to let out your story will change your life.

Sharing your story is much like letting the air out of the basketball you're trying to submerge in the pool. Once you share it, the air (power) goes out of the story, and you no longer have to fight to keep it submerged. Memory is a strange, fickle thing. Often when folks share their stories, they realize that their fears morph from the Great and Powerful Oz to a short man on a stool pulling levers. Telling our stories deflates the power they have over us.

Recently, I met a woman with a sordid, painful story. She couldn't meet my eyes, and when she spoke I had to lean in close because of her whisper. Such shame permeated her awful, dreadful memories. In the space of sixty minutes, the story halted, then poured out. I listened. I felt so privileged to be a part of this painful, beautiful moment with her. The downcast eyes upturned at the end of her story. When she knew I understood, and when she saw that her story was much more universal than she expected, something softened and blossomed in her. I can't prove this, of course. All I can offer is my observation. When I met her, she was a timid wisp of a woman. When we parted, her eyes had dance in them, and she smiled.

## THE PRESSURE TO KEEP SILENT

Some of you reading this grew up in a generation that had an unspoken rule: Never tell your story, particularly if it made a family member look bad—an unwritten, powerful code that hogtied you to secrecy. The problem with this shame-based model is that it didn't allow for truth. And healing seldom comes unless truth is attached. You may have had siblings whose silent pressure kept you from spilling the story. Or your parents may have threatened, maybe not overtly, but you felt the pressure to conform, to be quiet. I've heard from many sixty-, seventy- and eighty-year-olds who grew up in this system and are now finding freedom for the first time by sharing their stories with a trusted person. Yet many go to their graves with the secret on the tip of their tongues, never released.

Some of you are afraid to tell your story because it will seem like you've dishonored your parents by doing so. Mind if I send a little freedom your way? The Hebrew word for honor (as in "Honor your mother and father") is *kabbed*,[8] which means to give weight to. It means we hold in high regard the office of motherhood and fatherhood. We respect the fact that God placed us in our families, and we remain grateful for the role they had in our lives. This was hard for me for a long time. While I was still in the throes of healing, I could not see the positive traits of my parents. But as I've walked the healing journey, I've begun to "give weight to" the better memories that have surfaced after I've had more healing. (Consequently, you'll know when you've healed a bit when good memories start to resurface.)

So, you might be asking, what if I tell the truth? Won't I get in trouble? Won't it mean that I am no longer honoring my parents?

Jewish rabbinical literature had what they called, "the problem of the wicked father."[9] If our parents asked us to do things contrary to God's law, we are then allowed to honor God first. This sets us free to kindly and graciously tell the truth about the past. It doesn't mean we amplify it and share it with the world, but it does give us freedom to share with a trusted friend about when our parents didn't exemplify godly behavior.

But even beyond the problem of the wicked father, we can find assurance as we look at Jesus and how He interacted with his earthly parents. His obedience cost his parents dearly. His choices, completely and utterly aligned with His heavenly Father, hurt his parents. And yet, He did what He did anyway.

Jesus even disregarded his earthly mother when she wanted to meet with Him. "Then Jesus's mother and brothers came to see him. They stood outside and sent word for him to come out and talk with them. There was a crowd sitting around Jesus, and someone said, 'Your mother and your brothers are outside asking for you.' Jesus replied, 'Who is my mother? Who are my brothers?' Then he looked at those around him and said, 'Look, these are my mother and brothers. Anyone who does God's will is my brother and sister and mother'" (Mark 3:31-35, NLT). He elevated our true family as those who follow after God, not simply our earthly family.

Jesus also said that sometimes, because we follow Him, we will become estranged from our families. "Don't imagine that I came to bring peace to the earth! I came not to bring peace, but a sword. 'I have come to set a man against his father, a daughter against her mother, and a daughter-in-law against her mother-in-law. Your enemies will be right in your own household!' If you love your father or mother more than you love me, you are not worthy of being mine; or if you love your son or daughter more than me, you are not worthy of being mine" (Matthew 10:34–37, NLT).

To be honest, there have been times in my life when I've wanted to be free, to be able to live my life without the heartache associated with family. Yet, Jesus reminds us that even if our parents (or other family members entangled in our sexual abuse story) act as enemies to us and to God, we still have a responsibility to love them, pray for them, and ask God for guidance as we set boundaries with them. Jesus said, "But I say, love your enemies! Pray for those who persecute you!" (Matthew 5:44, NLT).

Love and prayer will look different to everyone reading this. For me? It means daring to love someone through telling the truth in the gentlest way. I don't feel it is love to allow someone to live in unreality, or to continue unchecked in lying or hiding. For a better perspective on this, consider picking up, *Changes that Heal* by Dr. Henry Cloud and John Townsend. That book transformed the way I lived. For years I kept quiet, believing that silence equaled honor. Eventually I began to see that silence actually meant enabling bad behavior and unreality. I learned to set appropriate boundaries with family members, which, to be honest, didn't go over well. I still smart from the resistance I've received. But I am so much happier and healthier as a result.

I love the freedom in what David Stoop writes: "It is healthy, not dishonoring, to acknowledge that our parents failed us, hurt us, damaged us in some way— especially if we are doing so for the sake of forgiving them. We do neither our parents nor ourselves any honor by denying reality, eliminating the possibility of forgiveness, and locking ourselves into dysfunctional patterns of thinking and acting."[10] With untruth and an inability to say what really happened, we close the door to true forgiveness. We cannot forgive what "didn't happen." Telling the truth is a brave act that actually flings wide the door to reconciliation and forgiveness. Keep in mind that truth-telling doesn't guarantee relationship—in many cases, it alienates. But you'll never know if the other person is willing to walk toward you if the truth doesn't first sit between you.

## WHY TELL THE TRUTH?

Why this push toward truth? Why not bury our story and hide it? Because we will not heal without truth and light. Satan, the father of lies, flaunts our worthlessness in the hidden, dark places. It's only when we are brave enough to share what really happened that he can no longer taunt us and holler our inferiority. "He was a murderer from the beginning. He has always hated the truth, because there is no truth in him. When he lies, it is consistent with his character; for he is a liar and the father of lies" (John 8:44, NLT). And those lies thrive in our minds, particularly if we haven't let the story out. They become bigger than a monster, untamed, unchecked. But look what happens when we speak the truth in the light: "And you will know the truth, and the truth will set you free" (John 8:32, NLT).

Truth always frees.

Hiding keeps us in darkness.

Anne Lamott famously penned, "Risk being unliked. Tell the truth as you understand it. If you're a writer, you have a moral obligation to do this. And it is a revolutionary act—truth is always subversive."[11]

Perhaps that's why we shrink from telling our stories. We don't want to risk being "unliked," particularly by the people who shaped us growing up. Or perhaps the fear of what will happen in the aftermath of our telling is far too great. We cannot see freedom because fear looms larger. Maybe one of our coping mechanisms plucked from a chaotic childhood is control, so to tell the truth means we invite chaos. Or maybe we're like King David after his indiscretion with Bathsheba and the subsequent killing of her husband: we think hiding works.

Some of you reading this book have already boldly and bravely told your stories. I applaud you. Some of you have overshared your story because you're seeking for someone to validate your experience. Or you've bottled it up too long, or retell it again and again for attention. I did that when I first started talking about my sexual abuse—as if I'd been uncorked and I couldn't help but let the desperation flow. I have such compassion and grace to those of you in that stage of healing. Some of you shared your story once, but weren't believed. That happened to me, too. Had I let that prevent me from further sharing my story, I would not be who I am today. The best way to share a story, particularly such a sensitive and painful story like sexual abuse, is to find a safe person to share it with.

## SAFE PEOPLE

Even if you've shared and been shut down, dare to share your story with a safe person. For some of you, your safe-person assessment tool is wonky, and you keep ending up with unsafe folks who make things worse after you share your story (either by unbelief, blame, or exploitation). If that's the case, consider reading *Safe People* by Cloud and Townsend. That will help you retrain the way you see relationships to find truly safe people. Counselor Lucille Zimmerman offers, "Safe people open the door for you to share more—at your own pace. They listen rather than telling you where you are. They are caring rather than offering trite answers or religious platitudes (for example, 'Trust Jesus'). They invite. Rather than closing you down, they open you up."[12]

**Safe people . . .**

- Ask clarifying questions.
- Don't jump to conclusions.
- Aren't passive-aggressive.
- Empathize with you, not needing to interject their own story of doom to one-up you.
- Encourage other relationships.
- Honor and encourage your relationship with God.
- Want what is best for you and your healing journey (don't have their own healing agenda, or pressure you to heal their way).

- Aren't domineering.
- Tell the truth, even if it's painful, but they tell it in a winsome way.
- Offer grace.
- Are self-aware.
- Reveal their flaws.
- Aren't defensive.
- Apologize, even before they're caught.
- Take responsibility for themselves.
- Work on their own issues.
- Want to learn from their mistakes.
- Accept blame.
- Avoid gossip.
- Are humble, teachable.
- Have a positive influence over your life.
- Have proven themselves trustworthy over a period of time.
- Are the same person in different situations—consistent.
- Applaud your growth.
- Don't try to be your parent or the Holy Spirit.
- Love freedom.
- Don't demand trust—instead they earn it by consistently acting honorably.

I healed because I found safe people in college who listened to me, loved me, validated the horror of my story, and prayed me toward health. They assured me my worth wasn't tied to the violation. In sharing my story, I opened up communication for deeper discussion within my friendships, often discovering that so many others had my same story, different verse. Dr. Henry Cloud affirms our need for community as we seek healing, "Without a solid, bonded relationship, the human soul will become mired in psychological and emotional problems. The soul cannot prosper without being connected to others."[13]

As I look back on my healing progress, I see now that it slowed to an almost halt in my twenties. Why? Because I shut my mouth for a decade. I believed, wrongly, that my healing was complete, and that I would no longer be shackled by the sexual abuse story. While much healing had happened, I had a long way to go, which accounts for the major fall-apart that happened in my thirties.

Sharing your story won't magically heal you, but it is an important first step on the long and beautiful and sometimes-rocky road to healing. I wish I could offer a panacea to you, that if you share your story, you'll automatically share it with a person of peace who loves you through healing. That as the result of that one precious encounter you'll be healed once and for all, and be able to think of sex as holy and amazing. As I've mentioned earlier, nothing guarantees complete healing this side of eternity. We wait, we groan, we hurt in this life, sometimes disillusioned, sometimes clinging to a shred of hope.

But if we long for wholeness, we can't underestimate the power of telling our stories. University of

Texas professor Dr. James Pennebaker researched the difference between rape and trauma survivors telling their stories versus keeping them secret. "The research team found that the act of not discussing a traumatic event or confiding it to another person could be more damaging than the actual event. Conversely, when people shared their stories and experiences, their physical health improved, their doctor's visits decreased, and they showed significant decreases in stress hormones."[14] Pennebaker's studies can also help those of you who are deeply terrified about telling your stories to others. The bulk of his research deals in expressive writing.[15] He found that journaling about a painful event fifteen to twenty minutes a day during a one-week period positively affected victims' physical and mental health. So if you're afraid to share the trauma from your past, consider writing about it, getting the words out, so you can begin to heal.

## VULNERABILITY

Though we may learn to tell (or write) our story, find freedom, and even seek to help others heal, we still can't fully escape the pain. We ask God to remove the grief, but for whatever reason, the sting remains. God replied to Paul's request that a painful thorn in his life be removed by saying, "But he said to me, 'My grace is sufficient for you, for my power is made perfect in weakness.'" Then Paul responded with an audacious vow to be vulnerable: "Therefore I will boast all the more gladly of my weaknesses, so that the power of Christ may rest upon me. For the sake of Christ, then, I am content with weaknesses, insults, hardships, persecutions, and calamities. For when I am weak, then I am strong" (2 Corinthians 12:9–10, ESV).

When Paul tells his story, he boasts about his weaknesses, his vulnerability. Why? Because that thorn reminds him of his need for Christ. He wouldn't know God's strength without it. I can honestly say that the sexual abuse I encountered has weakened me. Sharing it publicly is painful, sometimes excruciating. But I tell my story not to point to the devastation as much as I can highlight God's strength. Maybe that's why all of us should share our stories.

Dr. Brene Brown has spent her adult life researching shame, and in that research stumbled upon something extraordinary—vulnerability is something we shouldn't flee, but embrace. "To feel is to be vulnerable. To believe vulnerability is weakness is to believe that feeling is weakness. To foreclose on our emotional life out of a fear that the costs will be too high is to walk away from the very thing that gives purpose and meaning to living."[16]

Paul didn't shrink from his vulnerability. He walked through many tumultuous events, one of which brought him near death. I believe there's something profound here for sexual abuse victims: "We think you ought to know, dear brothers and sisters, about the trouble we went through in the province of Asia. We were crushed and overwhelmed beyond our ability to endure, and we thought we would never live through it. In fact, we expected to die. But as a result, we stopped relying on ourselves and learned to rely only on God, who raises the dead. And he did rescue us from mortal danger, and he will rescue us again. We have placed our confidence in him, and he will continue to rescue us. And you are helping us by praying for us. Then many people will give thanks because God has graciously answered so many prayers for our safety" (2 Corinthians 1:8–11, NLT).

First note that Paul didn't refrain from telling his scary story. He told it raw and real. He didn't use platitudes to cover up the stress. No, he said he was crushed and overwhelmed. Have you ever looked back on your sexual abuse story and felt that way? Crushed and overwhelmed—exactly what I felt. And there were times, like Paul, that I felt like the abuse had put a sentence of death within me. Like the thorn, this desperate situation pressed Paul to lean on God instead of his own wit and wherewithal. That tenacious grit inspires me, and sometimes it makes me tired. Sometimes I don't want to endure more healing. Sometimes I want to pretend it wasn't my story. Sometimes I want a new identity, divorced from "sexual abuse survivor." But as a truth-telling girl, I can't.

The beautiful part of these verses comes in this line: "We have placed our confidence in him, and he will continue to rescue us. And you are helping us by praying for us." First, Paul has confidence that God will absolutely deliver him afresh. He has hope. But he has also invited the Corinthian church to share in his story. He had shared it for the sake of prayer, so they could enter into the trial with him.

## COMMUNITY ALSO HEALS

Consider this: Paul talked about his burden in Asia, which was most likely caused by dissension and people being naughty. But he didn't let that negative experience with people taint his ability to share his need with other safe people. That's a picture of our abuse. People have been utterly and horridly naughty toward us. What happens, often, is that we let those perpetrators color the way we see the entirety of humanity, even safe people. The very difficult truth is that God often asks us to step into what has, in the past, wounded us. We are harmed and maimed by community, but the only healthy way through is to heal in community.

It seems unfair.

It seems counterintuitive.

It seems foolhardy.

But telling our stories will always involve at least one other human being, with ears to hear, and hopefully prayers to pray.

What so often happens is that we build a wall against all people because of the choices of perpetrators in our past. We shrink away, preferring isolation to community, because we feel safer that way. But doing that isn't safe. Why? Because isolation breeds bitterness and anger and a crazy brain. We even erect giant walls against our spouses because we cannot let ourselves be truly known. It's just too frightening. We shrink from telling the story of what is going inside us because we want to protect ourselves at any cost.

I'm not talking about protection from enemies or perpetrators or people who are unsafe. Paul didn't ever shrink from pointing out people like that and exposing them and distancing himself from them. No, I'm talking about what Paul does next: he entrusts himself to trustworthy people. He embraces safe community for the sake of finding camaraderie and support.

## THE WORD PICTURE THAT REVEALED ME

During my late twenties, when I'd stopped telling my story and preferred to think myself fully healed, my husband told me a story that broke my heart. (He alluded to it earlier.) He said he felt like I was pacing on a high dive, while he and the kids splashed in the pool below. I walked back and forth on that diving board, but never jumped in. Instead, I walked over to the pool's edge and put my toe in the pool, never entering into the lives of my new family. I'd chosen isolation over community in my quest to convince myself that I had already been healed. I'd protected myself all right—so much so that I no longer attached emotionally to the ones I loved the most.

That powerful word picture may be yours. Because of sexual abuse, you've kept everyone, even the good, safe people God has blessed you with, at a distance. You've not entered into their lives on a deep emotional level. You're too afraid to. You've had far too much pain, and you feel your heart will break in two if you risk again, only to be pounced upon.

You may even feel like I felt at the dentist last week. She asked if my bum tooth had been acting up since our last visit, and truth-telling me (not!) said all was well. Why? Because I'm terrified of root canals, thanks to an evil Endontist stateside and a long-drawn out root canal in France that scared the bejeebers out of me. I'd rather pretend my tooth didn't hurt, hoping the pain would magically lessen. Deep down, I know my terrible lie only delays the inevitable, and had I been truthful in the moment, I would no doubt save myself much pain in the process.

I share this to say that we're all like this on some level. We'd rather deny the pain we have, try to pretend it doesn't exist, rather than root out (pun intended) the dysfunction now. We let the fear of future procedures frighten us from being healthy now. The problem is, my tooth will eventually die, and I'll have to have the procedure anyway. May as well get it over with now. And in terms of your emotional pain from the sexual abuse, hear me when I say it will not get better. Entropy will have its way in the silence and will morph into something much worse.

Tell it like it is.

Own your pain.

Acknowledge that it exists and that it is a part of you.

Because, truly, you won't be whole if your heart is aloof and "safe." I wish I could reattach you to your life and the people who love you the most. But that will have to be your choice. And it starts with the simple act of bravery: telling your story to safe people, then entrusting the rest of your story to the God who continues to heal you.

## BE BRAVE FOR THEIR SAKE

You might feel it selfish to pursue all this healing. Bravery appears narcissistic in a way—after all it's all about you-you-you telling your story to get better. As you consider courage, shift away from yourself a moment. If you can't heal for yourself, and you worry that focusing on it is either unnecessary or selfish, choose to be brave for those who love you. Heal for their sake. The people who love you long for you to be whole, renewed, fully alive. They want what is best for you. They want to see you soar, not sour.

But they also need you—the real, vulnerable you. Sexual abuse typically causes victims to disengage— to stay aloof from life so life can't bludgeon us again. The problem is, our loved ones cannot have a genuine relationship with a detached person. They can't engage with an untethered ghost. They certainly can't truly love us if we're not really ourselves, but a facsimile. That's what makes the healing journey so blessedly brave. It involves heroic risk, daring to dig deeper into our hurts, being willing to share our struggles, sharing our stories with the desire to be set free. We do this for others—to love them well. We do this for ourselves— to taste freedom again or for the very first time.

Healing, my friend, is pure bravery.

## FROM PATRICK:

To ask someone who has been abused to share their story with you can be an overwhelming challenge. As Mary says, there is so much shame and self-condemnation that goes along with being a victim of abuse. Add to that the almost pathological mistrust of people, it is a recipe for bottling it up and hoping it never surfaces.

When I got married, I knew of Mary's abuse, but I didn't know the details or the extent—much of which she only remembered as time went on. Perhaps you are married to an abuse victim but you didn't know that was part of his or her past. Perhaps your spouse has never even shared anything about it with you. You want desperately for your spouse to be healed and you know that if they can share it with you, they can begin that journey. So what can you do?

The most important thing is to become someone who is trustworthy. If you are not someone your spouse trusts, she will never truly share her heart with you. If you don't treat her emotions and story with respect, if you refuse to change your behavior when it causes "triggers" in your spouse, then you will never have the intimacy you hope for.

I didn't learn the lesson about being trustworthy until we had been married about twelve years. That seems like a long time, but I had some growing up to do. The way Mary eventually found me to be trustworthy was based on at least these four things:

1. I didn't change the subject when she decided to talk about her abuse—I actively listened and also validated her feelings.
2. I began to own my own "stuff." It was important that she knew I was not perfect. It was important that she knew I was not her counselor but a fellow-struggler.
3. I was vulnerable too. This is a hard one for guys—at least this guy—because vulnerability is a sign of weakness. I believed it could be used as a weapon against me. It takes a lot of trust to be vulnerable.
4. I actively changed the way I behaved if it was causing her to remember her abuse. If there were things I did that triggered her, I had to consistently and intentionally work at not doing those things. This can only happen with humility and a deep concern for the other person—in other words, selflessness.

Following these four steps may be only the beginning. Each person and couple are different with unique dynamics. Perhaps there is a lot of confession and forgiveness that needs to happen on your part. Perhaps there are circumstances that need to change in order for communication to truly begin. Perhaps professional counseling is needed. To be a person available and trustworthy means you are willing to do anything for that person, and no matter what comes out of her mouth, you will neither run away nor share it with anyone else.

# CHAPTER
# 4

# EMBRACE GRACE

## STOP COMPARING THE WORST IN YOU
## TO THE BEST IN OTHERS

*"The Lord be with your spirit. Grace be with you."*

1 TIMOTHY 4:22, ESV

A friend of mine once gave me the kernel of a beautiful illustration. It's helped me heal because of its sheer simplicity and visual representation of healing.

Imagine you're standing in the middle of a street in a non-HOA neighborhood. Some homes have immaculate yards. One in particular preens. The homeowner's lawn makes golf courses jealous. He kneels before it, scissors in hand, hair-cutting stray blades of grass. The flowers, carefully planted behind rock edging, never violate their boundaries. They are a wash of color, well trimmed, neat. The shrubbery is Disney-esque, cut into manicured shapes. The sidewalk is tinted gunmetal gray, not a stain or pock in sight. Hanging pots drip cascades of green and flora, never dried out, always watered and vibrant.

But next door? Oh dear, next door. The yard is opposite in every way. A tangle of weedy mess. There's rumored to be an old transmission buried in the plant ruins. No lawn preens, just patches of wheat-like grass, interrupted by barren earth, dotted by fire ant mounds. An old bike rusts near the mailbox, which leans southward. Weeds twine through the yard, kudzu-crazy, and the hanging pots house critters.

Go ahead, compare the two yards. One is Yard of the Month material. The other, had there been an HOA, would be courting liens and fines.

But look a little closer at the messy yard. In the corner, if you crane your neck just so, you can see a tiny patch of earth weeded, and a single zinnia posing wildly, joyfully, soaking in the mid-afternoon sun. Unbeknownst to the neighbors, a young girl, tired of the mess that is her parents' yard, has taken pity on their patch of suburban earth, and made one corner beautiful. It took supreme effort, gutting out vine roots, adding a little potting mix, planting one solitary seed, watering it daily, praying for growth. Perhaps that zinnia is all the more stunning because of where it thrives. I think so.

Here's the truth: your yard is a mess. I know this is supposed to be a hopeful book, a book that helps you grow beyond disarray, but I wouldn't be loving you well if I didn't tell you this. The yard of your life has been invaded by pests, weed seeds, invasive plants, and all sorts of riffraff. The sexual abuse you've experienced has set you back, has marred your spot on this earth. It's not fair. It stinks. And it makes life seem impossible to you. But it happened, and here you are surrounded by a jungle of pain.

## STOP COMPARING

The problem comes when you look at the manicured yard next door and think you're a huge failure because you don't trim your grass with scissors. You look at the solitary zinnia you planted with disdain because it's everything the neighbor's yard is not. You cannot see the beauty or the progress because you're comparing yourself to a man who started out with a perfect, beautiful yard in the first place. The problem is we tend to compare our worst traits with the best traits in others. This kind of correlation leads to extreme defeat, making us want to give up the healing journey completely.

Other problems come when your spouse expects a perfect yard from you. If he or she does, you con-stantly live a frustrated, guilty, impossible life because no matter how you dig up your yard, it will never look pristine.

Here's the beauty, though. Redemption shines brightest on the darkest of canvasses. That little zinnia is proof of how far you've come. It may not seem like you've healed much, but since you've had so much more to overcome than others, your redemption beams all the more. Take a moment to gaze at its simple brilliance. Rejoice in how far you've come.

Stop looking at pristine yards.

Stop trying to act like folks who never had sexual injury.

Instead, find a small patch of earth and start working it, finding contentment in small bursts of growth.

If you are a spouse or friend who is reading this book, acknowledge each milestone a sexual abuse victim reaches—each weed eradicated, every seed planted, even a solitary bloom. Noticing even the smallest of advances and victories will do more to heal your loved one than expecting perfection.

## TEND YOUR YARD

Jesus came to messy-yarded folks like me, like you. He also said this painful truth, "I tell you the truth, unless a kernel of wheat is planted in the soil and dies, it remains alone. But its death will produce many new kernels—a plentiful harvest of new lives" (John 12:24, NLT). Death doesn't seem like a blessing, does it? But from the pain of that death comes exquisite life—a multiplied life.

You don't need a whole yard. You don't need perfection. You just need one seed and a big God of grace.

## A STORY OF SHAME

In grace, we all need to learn how to offer ourselves unmerited favor. This doesn't come easily to me, particularly in the arena of sex. As I mentioned earlier, when I was in my teens, I struggled with a pornography addiction long before the Internet proliferated it and made it accessible. Besides that, I was a girl (still am), and I'd only known of boys dealing with this issue. The problem? My home had pornographic books tucked into bookshelves, and I, a sexually damaged girl, had a seemingly inbred fascination with those books. I knew what I read was crooked, but this was before I met Jesus, before I understood the true nature of grace, before I even realized my yard was overgrown.

So when I met Jesus, I assumed this consuming of pornographic material would hereby cease. I'd no longer read this degrading, dark stuff. But I still wanted to, and my consuming fascination blossomed in the midst of the "Thou Shalt Not." Imagine how awful I felt that as a Christian, I was still addicted to porn. I did everything I could to shame myself into not looking. I punished myself if I strayed. I took cold showers. I fasted. I promised God one hundred million times that I would stop, only to return to it again and again. The shame nearly killed me. I believed because of it that I had become unregenerate, that I'd be one of those believers who were carnal and didn't really mean my conversion. I worried I had blasphemed the Holy Spirit. I certainly knew that God hated me and was gravely disappointed in me.

On the outside I looked like Suzie Christian, but on the inside, I carried this shameful secret with me. I assumed no one else struggled as I did, and I counted myself a reprobate. I lacked assurance, to put it mildly. Part of the aftermath of my sexual abuse was this fundamental belief that I had to earn a spot on God's green earth, which meant achieving a lot, but also meant never messing up. I wrote lists for myself to become perfect, desperate to curry the Almighty's favor. But because I believed that I had no worth, nothing I did satisfied.

Looking back on it, especially now that I'm a parent, I see how lost and needy I was. I have such compassion for that Mary. She just needed love. She needed a home that didn't have pornography in it in the first place. She needed nurture, not violation.

During this time of struggle (which I wrote about in *Thin Places*), I visited my grandparents in another state. There, my grandmother caught me reading a naughty magazine, and the shame overwhelmed me. Then on the way home from the airport, my mom let me know how icky it was to find my stash of books crammed between my bed and wall. She and her boyfriend had taken my vacation time as a green light to re-sheetrock my room. And that's when she found the books. She said something like, "Imagine how embarrassed I was when he found those books, Mary." I shrunk into myself, red-faced, red-souled. Shamed beyond words. Smaller than a dust mite.

I didn't know how I'd get over that scene in my life. It cemented all my fears about myself. That I was dirty. Unclean. Shameful. That I was utterly warped when it came to sexuality. That I was gross and truly unworthy of love or affection or tenderness.

## TELLING THE SECRET

Thank God, grace eventually burst through. It didn't flourish when I nursed my wounds in isolation. It arrived when I finally let out my secret addiction. It felt like penance to get it out the first time, only to discover I wasn't alone. I had felt like the dirtiest girl on the planet, but once I shared my struggle with a friend, I realized how universal the struggle toward sexual wholeness is for so many of us. In that circle of community, she spoke words of grace and forgiveness over me. And little by little, that scary addiction ebbed away.

It's still there, lurking inside. I see it when I read a novel that's too salacious. I have to put it down, get it out of my house. It takes very little time to move from normalcy to racy in my heart, and as I work to see sex as beautiful (it's still a struggle), I have to discard literature that cheapens and degrades it. For my sake. That being said, I know pornography isn't only a sexual abuse survivor's struggle. We are all bombarded with constant imagery. And we all have a daily choice about whether we'll welcome it into our yard or not. Be cautious, though. Pornography is like a morning glory vine—it takes over everything and is excruciating to uproot.

## THE MYTH OF PERFECTION

The great equalizing truth is that no matter who you are—sexual abuse victim or not—the idea of a pristine yard is a myth. It doesn't exist. We all have problem weeds. We all struggle to maintain a manicured life. We all have pain and sin marring the beauty. We're all messy. But thanks be to God, He graces the messy.

My yard is not pristine. I've got weeds aplenty that life dealt me (and I planted myself). But my little patch of zinnias has morphed into a wild English garden, a stunning picture of grace in my life. I'm still not keen on offering myself that grace, but I'm learning. That's my prayer for you today as you finish reading this chapter, that you'd take a moment to look over how far you've come on this sexual abuse recovery journey. Don't focus so much on the weeds or the supposed perfection of other people's yards, or you'll miss the little patch of earth you've seen flourish. That's grace. That's progress.

## FROM PATRICK:

One of the things Mary and I figured out early on was how to fight fair. You may ask yourself what that has to do with grace. As it turns out, quite a bit. I know Mary would have a difficult time if she felt abandoned or if she felt belittled. Sure, nobody likes that, but in the midst of an argument if I did something that made her feel that way, then all the work she had done in the journey of healing from her abuse would take several steps backward.

So I made a couple of vows to myself and to her. No matter how mad I got at her, I would never leave the house and drive off. I may storm into the other room and firmly close the door, but I would not leave so she knew I would return. I vowed I wouldn't swear at her or call her names. It helped that I grew up in a house where my mom and dad didn't argue this way. But if in the middle of a disagreement I would have called her a name, it would become a bequeathed "title" that could not be undone—validating what she had told herself in the past. We have friends who argue this way, and perhaps it works for them, but for us? A deal-breaker.

That is not to say I am a saint when it comes to our arguments. But it is a measure of grace that no matter how angry or upset I may be, I have not crossed that line. It is only by God's grace that she can know that regardless of the issue at hand, I love her enough and she can trust me enough that I will not abandon her or belittle her.

# CHAPTER
# 5

# SEEK HELP

## YOU HAVE MORE COUNSELORS
## THAN YOU REALIZE

*"Those who take advice are wise."*

PROVERBS 13:10, ESV

Once I told my mom that I'd been sexually abused, she encouraged me to get counseling. I resisted for a year or so, mainly because I was a new Christian and I didn't know if the counselor would gel with my faith. But eventually I did see a therapist a few times, only to realize that the counselor's pet theory about everything stemmed from alcoholism. She gave me several books about being an adult child of an alcoholic, which were mildly helpful (at least in understanding a dysfunctional home) but had relatively nothing to do with sexual abuse or the shame I carried.

For several years, particularly in college when I'd experienced so much healing from friends and church members who prayed me through, I believed counseling was unnecessary, and sometimes thought it evil. (This was during my hyper-vigilant stage of Christianity where I saw New Age under every self-help rock, when I dutifully threw my Tears for Fears albums away because they were "secular.") College, as I mentioned, ushered in the decade of Mary Being Okay, where I was henceforth and forever healed of all that awful sexual abuse stuff. I started my marriage, had my kids, and went on my Mary way.

Only my Mary way wasn't good enough.

As I mentioned, I struggled with sex, with detaching, with body image as my form changed with each child, with exhaustion in raising my children. I worried constantly (obsessively) that I was a terrible mommy. I kept picturing my children in counseling years later saying things like, "I'd be okay today if it hadn't been for my crazy mother."

## FRIENDS AS COUNSELORS

I started unraveling right around my thirtieth year. Thankfully, God sent a counselor of sorts in the shape of an amazing woman named Kathy. She was older, wiser, and full of Holy Spirit insight. I shared some of my darkest, deepest, most painful secrets with her, and she dared to pray me through toward healing.

My marriage during that time felt distant and painful. Having two children by then, we hadn't navigated the change well, and I found my husband more aloof and more disdainful of me. I reasoned it was all my fault, for not being sexy enough, not having sex enough, not being everything he wanted from me. This panicked me. I ached for us to be close again, but nothing I did, including daring to initiate sex, worked. In retrospect, this seven-year itch tends to be a common stage of marriage, but I had no way of knowing that—having been a child of three divorces. The one thing that helped me through that painful season became a tenacious clinging to Jesus. I simply asked Him what He wanted me to do, and then I did it, despite the state of my marriage. This counsel from Jesus proved valuable to me, and my friend Kathy affirmed my decisions during this time.

During this period of my life, I started growing closer to another friend. She'd undergone some pretty scary changes in her life and had spent some time in counseling. I remember one conversation we had. She said something like, "My life has shrunk in the past few months. I am taking inventory of all my relationships. And I choose you because I know you're a good friend." That decision on her part and mine made way for one of the most healing relationships of my life. She became a counselor/friend.

She was the friend who sat across from me in a breakfast restaurant and unmasked something I hadn't been willing to admit about my father. I'd spent several minutes sharing about my struggle with my mom when she stopped me and said, "Mary, I've often found that it's the parent we don't talk about with whom we struggle the most."

I, of course, didn't believe her. No, my father was perfect. My hero. He loved me. He cared about me. When he died, my life imploded. My poor friend was fully and utterly mistaken, and I told her as much.

"Why don't you tell me more about him," she said.

I shared about the bathtub, me bathing him. The pictures he'd show me of askew, vacant-staring women, unclothed. The days with naked people parading through his house. The parties of more nudity.

"That is not love," she said.

Those four words became an arrow through my carefully constructed story. Mary had a hard life. Boys molested her. Her mother and stepfather didn't seem to notice. She felt unsafe, unwanted. But every other weekend, her father stole her away from all that. He rescued her. He loved her. He dignified her.

"Can't you see?" She looked me in the eyes. "He was grooming you."

Right there over eggs and toast and anguish, I wept, vision blurring. Finally able to speak, I said, "But if I admit that what my father did wasn't loving, then I have to admit no one really loved me."

She let my words hang in the café air between us. "Jesus is the hero of your story, Mary. Not your father." And like that, I saw the past more clearly. She had clarified something I'd not allowed myself to see. And I had to start over on my journey of healing.

Not all counseling happens in a counselor's well-apportioned office. Some of you can't afford counseling. Some of you are terrified of it. Some of you have been burned by counseling. My hope is that I can broaden your view of it. God often sends wise people into our lives at just the right moment to lure a new truth from us, or open our eyes to the need of healing. They affirm our stories, but love us enough not to let us dwell on them.

Living close to my family of origin and being in the midst of dysfunction kept me so entrenched in the pain that I couldn't see my story with proper perspective. It wasn't until I moved away that I began to have that perspective, but seeing my story from afar with clear eyes threatened to undo me. I needed help from trusted counsel. Because I knew no one in my city, I talked to a close friend's mentor. As I shared my story with this woman, I asked her if she thought I was depressed. I feared her answer. At that time, depression was taboo in the Christian community so I did not want to add pressure to my already struggling state.

"No," she said. "You're in a depressive state with difficulties around you, but you're not depressed."

This lifted a weight from me, and made me realize that what I was dealing with was hard, but not insurmountable. She prayed for me, and I felt a new kind of settled peace about the past, about my current situation. I had hope that I'd eventually heal from the pain of what happened back then.

## SPOUSES CAN BE COUNSELORS

My husband has been my most consistent counselor, particularly after we weathered our seven-year marriage problems. He once said to me, "Mary, I want the last half of your life with me to be amazing compared to the first years of your life." On so many levels he has kept that promise. He's pushed me to grow when I haven't wanted to. He's had to walk a very tenuous line in terms of our sexual relationship, trying to empathize and understand something he can't ultimately relate to (my sexual abuse) without letting me stagnate in my healing. It's a painful gift he gives to me when he shares he'd love me to be more affectionate, to be truly free. He knows it will most likely bum me out, but because he loves me and wants me to be alive and joyful, he sometimes presses so I'll see the need for healing in yet another area.

When we moved to Dallas so Patrick could attend seminary, we found out that one of the perks of being a student was that he or his spouse could receive complimentary counseling through their counseling program. By this time I had read every form of self-help book, including the vastly helpful *The Wounded Heart* by Dan Allender. But I was stuck. And I needed someone who knew more about the inner workings of the healing path to help me get to the next level of healing.

## THE BEAUTY OF PROFESSIONAL COUNSELORS

When I met with my first counselor, I told my story. One of the most healing things she said to me was, "So, you're telling me you've never had formal counseling."

I told her about the brief alcoholic family counseling I'd had in my teens. "Mostly I just had people pray for me," I said.

She shook her head. "With where you are, I cannot believe you haven't had years of counseling. It's remarkable."

Chalk one up to the power of really great friends and the beauty of prayer!

Those two years of counseling proved to be a gigantic blessing in my life. I dealt with my views of sex as dirty, asked hard questions and answered them, wrote letters that were never sent, worked on my relationship with my extended family, creating some of the first boundaries I'd ever erected, and started down a pathway toward healing.

Sometimes sexual abuse survivors get so stuck in our healing journey that we can't see our way through the jungle. We need a guide to hack away at the underbrush, someone either trained by college or trained by life or trained through trauma to offer insight and wisdom we simply don't have. Some of us need extensive PTSD therapies, including EMDR[17] to deal with the trauma of the past.

I first learned about EMDR (Eye Movement Desensitization and Reprocessing) from my counselor friend, Sue, who helped victims heal after sexual atrocities in Sierra Leone. The therapy involves recounting a tragic event—in our case, sexual abuse—while tracking eye movements, left to right. This is a severe oversimplification, but I've actually seen it happen accidentally in my own life. During long runs, I've recounted tragic events while my eyes looked left, then right, back and forth. After the run, I realized I'd reframed my memory—it no longer had an oppressive hold on me.

Diego experienced healing via EMDR after he couldn't find a way to process a sexually traumatic event. "I was nine years old. I took the bus with my friend after school, heading to his house as I usually did. His teenage brother appeared saying he had a cool new game to play. I followed him upstairs to his room. He closed the door and asked me to take my clothes off and go to his bed." Although the brother didn't have sex with Diego, the unwanted sexual touch scarred him. He kept it quiet.

Much later, after he was married, Diego shared this encounter with his therapist, wife, and sister. During an EMDR session he reframed the horrifying event, making peace with what happened—no longer traumatized by the memory. The irony is that Diego grew up in a good, stable family. "I had an almost perfect family. We were really close to each other. I had wonderful parents—yet this happened to me. So victims don't always come from 'messed-up' families." He also wants others to know that sexual abuse doesn't always encompass the entire sexual act. "The fact that my friend's brother did not get to actually have sex doesn't mean it wasn't sexual abuse."

Some of you reading this relate to Diego's story. You may be from a great family. Or you might've experienced unwanted sexual touch that didn't culminate in intercourse. The truth is sexual abuse happens to all kinds of people, from all different home lives, and in varying degrees of exploitation. No matter what your story, there may come a time when you need help getting through the pain—whether it be through EMDR or other avenues. You might need to attend intensive seminars, read books by experts, participate in a sexual abuse recovery group, or watch TED talks about the healing process. Some simply need to have coffee with a trusted friend who will dare to love us through our stories.

Counseling comes in many suitable forms, but as we welcome others into our healing journey, we'll find ourselves further along the path because of it. There's absolutely no shame in asking for help; in fact it shows your strength of character and your gutsy tenacity to get well.

# FROM PATRICK:

I don't really consider myself a very good counselor. Whenever I have counseled someone, usually in terms of biblical or pastoral counseling, it seems like the desired result rarely happens. I think the main reason for counseling failure is due to the reason people enlist a counselor. Some do it out of desperation, willing to do whatever it takes to change their situation. Some do it to validate their feelings and behaviors. Some do it begrudgingly as an item on a list to check off. In my limited experience it seems that what determines successful and unsuccessful counseling is the attitude and intentions of the one being counseled.

With Mary, when the moments come where I can speak into a situation in her life, I will try to gently nudge her that way. Sometimes it is not so gentle though.

One thing that demonstrates love to me is affection. My tank gets filled when Mary initiates affection—it doesn't have to lead to sex, but at least lets me know that she cares about me in that way. But giving affection is not easy for Mary; it does not come naturally. She has a difficult time receiving it as well.

So what should I do? Should I resign myself to an unaffectionate marriage or should I demand that every time I come home from work she gives me a big old kiss? Neither of these options are sustainable, although at times both approaches are necessary. There are times when I have to remember and realize that I cannot expect Mary to be affectionate the way I want her to. There are other times when I need to remind her that affection is important to me and she needs to know and be able to respond to that. I think "counseling" in this way offers both grace to grow at a pace the other can handle and also love that won't allow the other to stay the way they are. The success of this kind of counseling only goes as far as the person receiving it is open to it and responding to it.

# CHAPTER
# 6

# HEAL BY DESIGN

## HOW GOD MADE YOU IS HOW HE HEALS YOU

*"For we are God's masterpiece. He has created us anew in Christ Jesus, so we can do the good things he planned for us long ago."*

EPHESIANS 2:10, NLT

Ursula K. La Guin wrote, "A creative adult is a child who survived."[18] I love that. And I think that statement hints at the dynamic way God helps us heal from the past—in our own creatively bent way.

Consider your own story of coping, for that might give you a hint as to what your propensity is. For me, coping meant flying to the safety of trees high above me like a nested bird, creating my own stories while another story devastated me. When I was alone as a young kid, I invented an imaginary friend, DeeDee, to help me navigate my loneliness. I painted and drew and wrote little poems. I journaled. God used my creativity even then to protect me, shelter me, keep me sane.

Perhaps my creativity had a dark side, too. Maybe that's why pornography had such a pull to me—it felt foreign, different, enticing—those stories of men and women doing salacious things. Because of that, I've sometimes viewed my own creativity with fear and trembling. Because some of my father's writings were sometimes distorted and creepy, I've worried that my own literary experimentation would result in words that violate, rather than heal people.

## GOD USES YOUR BENT

Because you are shaped differently than me, you won't heal the same way I have. God always uses our uniqueness to bring healing. Some of us are nature lovers, and we experience the salve of healing in a pristine wilderness, a lake dazzling under the sun. Some will lose time in the midst of a musical piece. Some will work out their past and pain via physical exertion, running like Forrest Gump across America to meander through the loss of love. Some of us find healing through serving the poor, or identifying with them. Some of us paint away our pain. Others dig in the earth, experiencing the seasons of decay then rebirth, helping us heal with soil under our nails. The possibilities are limitless.

Ken Gire hints at the way God heals us when he writes, "We reach for God in many ways. Through our pictures and our prayers. Through our writing and our worship. And through them He reaches us."[19] Through the way God made us, He connects with us. Why? I'm not sure exactly, but I do know that I resonate more with lessons learned through beautiful words and stories than through lectures. My husband, on the other hand, started his healing journey in the aftermath of our church-planting time in France by reading a good theology book. We all have different dispositions, and God delights in that.

## GOD BRINGS HEALING IN A YOU-SHAPED WAY

God is the creator, and thus He is *our* creator. As image-bearers, we also create. Author Shauna Niequist eloquently affirms, "[God] was and is a million different things, but in the beginning, he was a creator. That means something for us, I think. We were made to be the things that he is: forgivers, redeemers, second chance-givers, truth-tellers, hope-bringers."[20] Can you catch the beauty in that? Satan came to destroy and de-story us. He cannot build or make, only tear down the masterpiece that God has created in us. Being unique reverses the injury, helps us reframe our memories, and gives us an outlet to process all that pain.

One ministry that embraces each person's unique design as a means to heal pain is Arts Aftercare. They strive to use the creative process to bring healing to trauma victims—particularly sex-trafficked victims. After hearing about one girl, Soraya, who could no longer speak because of the trauma she experienced in a Bangalore brothel, the band Jubilee felt the weight of the girl's sorrow. They asked probing questions. "What could the arts mean to someone who had been robbed of her voice? And how could that person's story change me as an artist? These were the questions that inspired the founding of Arts Aftercare. These questions continue to inspire us as we seek to become better artist-advocates for the millions still being enslaved, and to bring restoration and healing to those who have already been rescued."[21] As a result of introducing art therapy to victims around the world, they are seeing lives changed.

The sweet truth is that God has used my own design as a writer to bring about healing. Although I have more than twenty books to my credit now, I'm not a bestselling author. Not one of my titles has landed me on a "look at how cool Mary is" list. Each book I've written, including this one, has been God's pathway to heal me. Though I'd been wounded by words ("We'll kill your parents if you tell"), God saw fit to use words to heal me.

I experienced healing when I wrote my first novel *Watching the Tree Limbs*, a story about a young orphan girl, Mara, battling the worse kind of bully—someone who rapes her. Hmm, sound familiar? Though not entirely my story, writing my character's journey was an enlightening, yet painful exercise. As I wrote it, I drew from my sexual abuse. I saw the world through the eyes of my protagonist. I wanted to shrink back, to make her situation not so stark.

In the first draft of the story, I wrote safe. I kept my character detached in the aftermath of her abuse. (Ahh, detachment, how I love and embrace you so!) The substantive editorial letter I received from the novel's editor detailed the problem: I was not telling the truth about my character's reaction to the abuse. I argued back with something like, "But that's reality! Abuse victims don't react in the moment. They stuff."

She insisted that the reader needed to love the character, which meant that the young protagonist had to have emotional responses to the abuse—those reactions gave her humanity, vulnerability.

One of the most difficult experiences of my writing life was going back through the novel, assigning emotions to my character—the prickly feelings I'd been afraid to confront, the reactions I never permitted myself to experience.

Young Mara had very little emotional response to her daily life—a life fraught with abandonment by her aunt, the mystery of her parents' whereabouts, and sexual abuse at the hands of a neighborhood bully named General. My first draft:

> She twisted and turned in her sheets, entangling her sweaty self in them like a cocoon. She closed her eyes and longed for an adult embrace—of a fond touching from her mother or her father. For a moment, one tiny moment, she willed her parents into existence—parents who would hold her like the sheets held her now. Instead of fighting against the percale, she slowed her breathing and begged for sleep. And God, if You are out there, please let me find my voice in the nightmare.

In the final draft, I expanded the scene to give the reader a clearer picture of Mara's emotional landscape. I gave her the emotions I'd never been allowed to experience as a child. In my home, I should be happy always, certainly not traumatized or fearful or worried. I wasn't allowed to react normally to painful situations. So I assigned those emotions to Mara. The resulting healing has been one of the most profound of my life.

> She twisted and turned in her sheets, entangling her sweaty self in them like a straight jacket. She closed her eyes and longed for a hug—of a fond touching from her mother or her father. For a moment, one tiny moment, she willed her parents alive—parents who would hold her like the sheets held her now. Instead of fighting against the bedding, she slowed her breathing and begged for sleep.
> As she started to fall asleep, a tear trailed out of her eye. She wiped it, but another one came. Then

another. Before she could wipe them all away, a sob burst from her chest. She smashed her pillow to her mouth, suffocating her wail. Heaving chest, watering eyes, aching heart—all these combined into a display of weepy helplessness. She ached for Nanny Lynn to come back from heaven, to swoop down like a cowbird to rescue her from General. But no matter how much she cried, nothing would change. And this made her weep all the more until she heard footsteps.

Aunt Elma appeared in her doorway. "You crying? What for?"

Mara heard a tinge of tenderness in her aunt's voice. For a moment, she wanted to spill everything out. "I'm sad."

"Mara, how many times have I told you that Nanny Lynn, she ain't coming back, no matter how much you boo-hoo." Aunt Elma walked over to her bed and bent low. In a rare show of motherly attention, she smoothed the covers over Mara and stood. She shook her head.

Mara could see her wet eyes. She misses Nanny Lynn as much as I do. Maybe she'll understand if I tell her about General. Maybe that's love behind her eyes. "I know, but—"

"No buts about it. Get over it. I want no more tears about her. She's gone. You should be over her by now." She turned abruptly and shut the door behind her.

> Mara slipped her thumb in her mouth, thankful she hadn't spilled her words, worried if she didn't plug her mouth, she would.[22]

Another way God has chosen to heal me is through music. When I'm at my lowest, I've learned it's best if I turn on a playlist full of uplifting, positive songs. In the past, I'd wallow in minor key music, playing the songs over and over again, but now I gravitate toward happier beats. Perhaps this means I'm healing even more.

Stories through movies or the writings of others have also played a role in my healing. When Jenny in *Forrest Gump* hurled stones at that house where her greatest hurt occurred, and Forrest said that sometimes there aren't enough rocks, I bent into myself, agreeing with the words, hurling imaginary stones at the little white home that housed me when I was five. When Antwone Fisher (of the movie with that name) cries as his neglectful mother stares off into space, never answering his questions or uttering, "I'm proud of you, son," I understood, broke a bit, then teared up when the next scene showed Antwone loved and welcomed by his father's side of the family. When a movie churns emotions in me I've learned to pay attention and to ask why. In that asking, I recognize new tender spots that are mending—or need healing.

## AND YET, WE FEAR

Lately, I've again seen a shift toward more wholeness and healing as I've ventured into difficult territory in the blogosphere, the main scary blog being "The Sexy Wife I Can't Be" that proved to be the impetus for this book. I worried before I wrote that post and a series of follow-up posts, that people from my past would contact me. That fear is still real to me, forty-one years post abuse. And it is a founded fear. Once again, I did hear from someone who knew me back then. The e-mail lambasted me, questioned my story, pushed back against it. At first I mired myself in those words. But thankfully, this time, God had a surprise for me. My eldest daughter saw my demeanor shift when I read the e-mail and sighed heavily.

"What's wrong?" she asked.

"This," I said, and pointed to the e-mail.

She read it, then hugged me, then blessed me with praying words. She prayed the damaging words wouldn't have their desired effect. She prayed for protection for me. She prayed God would heal me again. And then she said amen.

God illuminated something powerful in that moment. One e-mail represented my family of origin—a family bent toward hiding. And my new family, the one I'd forged from the ashes of my past, desperate for Jesus to help me, represents who I am today. I am loved. I am surrounded by children and a husband who cheer for me. And I'm hugged by my word-loving daughter in the powerful medium of her prayer.

Soon after, I received this e-mail from my friend Holly. "So it seems the tone of your e-mails and blogs have shifted. In a good way. I sense such a hope, healing, transformation. Like, all these years of writing and speaking, exposing the nakedness, has finally fully healed you. (Jesus did it, but He used your creative outlet to process it.) I do know you have been intentional in some of it, but you couldn't do it with the authenticity that reads through the lines if you really weren't there yet. It's good. You are good. God is great! I love you."

Another word gift from the Almighty.

## JOURNAL YOUR PAIN

In terms of sexual abuse, it's also my unpublished words that have helped me work through my animosity. I've raged on paper. I've railed. I've questioned God and cried out through the nib of my pen. Sometimes I've hollered. I've learned in these interchanges that despite how we reach for God (words, songs, dance, exercise), His shoulders are big enough to take our wrath. He already knows our hearts anyway; we're not fooling Him by pretending we're hunky dory when our minds are actually helter-skelter messes. So there's no reason to be dishonest.

However you choose to express your hurt, do so with authenticity.

• • •

We're all shaped differently. We all heal differently. God has us on unique paths, and He uses our makeup to reach our hurting hearts, speaking to us in ways He knows we will hear.

## FROM PATRICK:

I am not by nature a very patient person. People who know me or have met me often describe me as "even-keeled" and "laid back." I am not sure where this comes from—perhaps from my general expressionless expression or my penchant for not showing emotions. In reality I can be very impatient. Just hang out with me sometime when I have to wait in line somewhere.

Impatience and healing are not very good bedfellows. There are times when I think, "How many times do we have to go through this? Hasn't she gotten over that yet?" I am sure if I am saying those things in my head, she is saying those things even more in her head. But people heal on different timetables. You never know what will help people get past their pain, and you never know how long it will take. And you never know the extent of the healing either.

I am in the medical field. One thing that happens when people have surgery is that it leaves a scar. It may not be a very big scar and it may not be a visible scar. You may look at the surface and think, That's no big deal, not realizing what kind of suturing happened under the skin. But even if things look fine on the outside, it can take a lot more time to heal the inside.

Many complications happen when we try to do too much too soon. The gift you can give your spouse is to get to know his or her uniqueness. How do they deal with things? What is their tendency—do they dismiss pain? Do they dwell and mire in their suffering? Do they revisit and fail to take steps to move on? Getting to know and anticipate how your spouse responds as they are healing will help immensely in your own patience for them, knowing best when to push a bit and best when to let things alone.

# CHAPTER
# 7

# DARE TO ASK

## UNLEASH GOD'S TRANSFORMING POWER
## THROUGH PRAYER

*"Elijah was as human as we are, and yet when he
prayed earnestly that no rain would fall, none fell for
three and a half years! Then, when he prayed again,
the sky sent down rain and the earth began to yield
its crops."*

JAMES 5:17–18, NLT

I woke up this morning heavy hearted. Writing this
book has dredged up all sorts of insecurities and
demons. Even last night Patrick and I had a disagreement, and we had to work through my own issues—
my fears of abandonment, my worries about not being

enough. Thankfully, we ended well. But during the conversation, he said, "I want you to finish that book soon." He can see what a toll these words have taken on me. I feel a tussle with the enemy, Satan, who obviously does not want me to write these words. And, in fact, it would be easier just to throw it away and move on.

In light of all that swirling around me, the phone rang. It was my friend Susie who prays for me. Her sweet interruptions are often God moments for me. Driving on her way to work, she felt an unction from Jesus and called me to pray. Her prayer brought tears to my eyes, tears of gratitude that God sees me and understands how hard this book is to write.

## PRAYER BY OTHERS

I wouldn't be here, in this place of healing, had I not been prayed for. Of any advice I can give about moving from sexually stressed to sexually joyful, the best is simply prayer, particularly when others pray for you.

I mentioned earlier that God sent many to pray for me during my college years. I can't count the times— probably hundreds, thousands. A great battle for my heart and life started then, a scary crossroads where I could give up, pursue a life of sexual deviance, angry at God, or turn to Him and ask for His deliverance. Sometimes the prayers were silent. Sometimes loud. Sometimes prophetic. Sometimes a joyful hush of God's presence. But each time someone prayed for me, I emerged from that place a different Mary—less harried, more settled, more healed.

God continued to send others to pray for me throughout the years. Among them was a ragtag band of women in a small Bible study who worshipped, interacted with each other and the Bible, and prayed together. It was during that study that one woman's prayer gave me hope that I would get through this pain and encouraged me to believe that someday I would announce the Lord to those who hurt.

Prayer has followed me all these years, helping me heal from things I didn't even know I needed healing from. I recount one story in *Thin Places* about a team of people who came to France and spent a long time praying for me. When they prayed, they instructed me to tell them which memory came up. I had a very specific image, but thought it too pedestrian, too simple. In it, I stood in a crib at four years old in the basement of my grandparents' home. I never gave that memory much weight, as it seemed a happy memory, a time when I was loved and wanted. I could see me in the basement during naptime, singing, while my grandmother's disembodied intercom voice told me to lie down. Eventually, even though I thought this a silly memory, I said out loud, "I'm standing in a crib, and I'm four years old."

Suddenly, I couldn't see straight. My chest tightened, and a huge sob erupted from so deep inside me, I wondered if I would explode. I realized in simply voicing the memory that I'd placed my hope of being wanted and loved by relatives in the wrong place. When my friend had gently reminded me that my father hadn't acted heroically, and hadn't loved me the way a good father should have, I moved all my eggs to my grandparents' basket. I reasoned, "Well, at least for one year of my life, when I lived with my grandparents, I was wanted and loved."

Except for the fact that I always felt in their way.

Except for those times when I'd have to play quietly in a stranger's master bedroom while my grandmother played Bridge.

Except for those strange baths where my grandmother would scrub my private parts raw.

I told them what I'd said to my friend, "But if I admit I wasn't even wanted by my grandparents, then not one soul wanted me. No one really loved me."

Through the prayer time, the anguish felt like a bowling ball on my chest. The weight, oh the weight, it would crush me. It wasn't until I saw a flicker of Jesus enter the basement of my memory, catch my glance from across the room, and lift me from the crib, did I realize that all along Jesus wanted me. He loved me. He cherished me, a little broken-down girl. The remade memory came to me as sheer gift, birthed through prayer.

Although that encounter didn't specifically have to do with my sexual abuse, it did deal with something I think many sexual abuse victims struggle with: our sense of worth. I've spent a lifetime (very tirelessly) trying to prove that I'm okay, that it's good that I take up space on this earth. I also struggled with questions about a good God versus what happened to me. In this prayer encounter, I began to see that my worth depended on Him, not me, and certainly not on other people's reaction to me. I also glimpsed His goodness in a way I hadn't before. Yes, the questions still linger about Him not rescuing me, but somehow they're softened around the edges.

## DARE TO ASK

Asking others to pray for you is not easy. It means that first you have to have praying friends, and then it takes nerve and bravery to actually ask. I wish I could pray for every single one of you reading this book because I'm convinced that God does amazing things through our prayers, not because of our clever phrases, but because of His care for us. He wants to heal us. He wants to help us. But He cannot if we turn our backs, if we don't avail ourselves to His body, the Church, if we live inside of ourselves, locked away by fear.

Asking for prayer is humiliating at times. It's humbling. It's sheer vulnerability, something sexual abuse victims typically do a lot to avoid. If asking someone to pray for you in the moment, right there, right then, terrifies you, start by asking a friend over e-mail if they'll pray for you today. As I was writing this chapter, a friend reached out to me via text asking me to please pray for her family. So today we're spending the day praying for each other, asking the God of heaven to please show Himself strong and available. I think we both need that vision of Him grabbing us from our lives and offering a great big hug.

## WRITE YOUR PRAYERS

Another way to walk through prayer is to write out your prayers to God in a journal. Share it all. He knows your anger and ambiguity anyway, right? Be honest. Rail. Rant. Fume. Cry. Question. God is absolutely big enough to shoulder your anger and bitterness. Your journals where you pray will become a chronicle of healing in your life. Much like it's hard to see how earning four cents on our savings means anything in only a month, we must give prayer time to compound. Don't expect instant growth. Over time, you can look back on what you've written, and see what God has done.

## SOME PRAYERS ARE ANSWERED; OTHERS ARE NOT

Last night Patrick and I talked about my disconnection from sex. I said, "I am finally beginning to connect during the act."

And like a breath of grace, he said, "I can tell. I see it." The progress toward connection has taken twenty-three years! And yet there is a different prayer that's remained unanswered for thirty-one years. Yes, it's discouraging when answers are slow in coming, but it's also wildly dynamic when you see progress, and you trace God's hand through your prayers and the prayers of others for you.

I have no great wisdom to offer you except a prayer I'll write for you. Place your name in this prayer. Live around in it for a bit. Kick the tires. May this prayer be an inauguration of your bravery to ask a living, breathing friend to pray you toward health. (Please note, to avoid the he/she issue, I'm using "they.")

Dear Jesus, I pray for _____ right now who holds this book. Please help them move beyond their fear of being found out toward a desire to be loved and prayed for by another. Please show _____ their worth, how precious, how amazing, how loved they are by You. Reassure _____ that no rant, rage, or question is too big for You. Would You show up in a painful memory? Would You begin the arduous process of healing that which has been stolen? Would You clean them from shame and guilt and blame and pain? Would You open the door ever so slightly toward health and joy? So much has been taken from _____. So much injustice and wrongdoing has attacked _____. It's not fair. It's awful, really. And _____ is left to pick up the pieces of other people's sinful choices. Oh that You would give _____ a new perspective on the past, to move from hating it to seeing it as a gift in light of Your redemption. Take the sexual abuse, heal the wounds, and do something marvelous and beautiful in _____ 's life today, tomorrow, and so many other tomorrows. When _____ feels used, or wants to withdraw, give strength and wherewithal. When having sex hurts or freaks or scares, please show up in that vulnerable place. Redeem the bed, Jesus. Redeem what's been stolen. Remake what has been broken. Rebuild that which has been disassembled. Retrain _____ 's mind to understand the gift of sex, instead of its obligation and exploitation. Use _____ 's experience to make them a light and beacon to others who have suffered. Rescue so _____ can be a rescuer. Redeem _____ 's marriage. Give _____ 's spouse holy, sweet, gentle understanding and grace. Provide praying friends. Do something new. Lift the depression. Restore that elusive hope that seems distant. We trust and rely on You, the Author of Life. Please, please, change us and start the healing journey, even if _____ is terrified. Amen.

## FROM PATRICK:

Whenever I am frustrated with Mary or come to the end of my rope in terms of how her healing is coming along, I have found it best to spend some time in prayer. This is a learned behavior for me. The last thing I feel like doing when in this state is to pray. I don't feel spiritual, and if I am honest, I usually don't care to hear what God has to tell me about my attitude. But I have found it to be much more productive for Mary and for me if I take the time to be alone with God and my thoughts. Although I have joined with my wife in prayer, it has been better for me if I am alone.

The subject of my prayer is for her. What this has done for me is to put me in a position of having to understand how best to pray for her. Not that she would "get over it" necessarily, although I do pray for her complete healing. More, that God would help me to consider how He views Mary. He tends to remind me of the gift she is for me and the vows I made before Him so many years ago. In sickness and in health. For better or for worse. These are covenant words, words breathed that outweigh how I might feel on a given day and provide direction and a foundation for my mind, heart, and soul. He reminds me that my expectations of Mary are limited and flawed. That He has much more in store for me through her.

So as in most things, when I come to Him about my wife, He tends to direct His (and my) attention more toward my issues. It is important that your spouse knows that you are praying for him or her. It does not have to be in a formulaic way before you both go to sleep (in fact we don't do that very often ourselves). But your spouse does have to see that God is working in you and that you are a cheerleader who is lifting them up consistently in prayer.

# CHAPTER
# 8

# TELL IT ALL

## HOW GUT-LEVEL HONESTY WITH OTHERS
## AND GOD MAKES SPACE FOR RESTORATION

*"But you desire honesty from the heart,*
*so you can teach me to be wise in my inmost being."*

PSALM 51:6, NLT

So young and naïve when we first married, it didn't occur to me to articulate my fear about sex to my husband-to-be. Perhaps if I'd been older or more in touch with exactly how I felt, I could've openly shared my reticence in a way that didn't sound small. Mostly I experienced a vague feeling of dread. (Apologies to Patrick; I'm sure that doesn't sound romantic!)

## DARE TO BE HONEST

A friend of mine, I'll call her Sarah, got engaged later in life after experiencing abusive marriages and many other situations of sexual victimization. This time she knew what she wanted, and was able to communicate with her fiancé, Davis, the turmoil inside her.

In her words, "We wanted to be pure with each other, so we had not fooled around at all. But when it came to the week before the wedding I realized I didn't know if I wanted to have sex on our wedding night. Or at all for a while because of all the sexual abuse I'd experienced. Up until then, I'd never really been able to say no. Sex was either expected or demanded or stolen. Although the night of my first marriage I was very eager for sex, there had still been that underlying expectation. So I told Davis I didn't know if I could give him what he most wanted on our wedding night. He wrote me back the most wonderful letter. He basically said that we didn't have to have sex on our wedding night and he wouldn't expect it. 'Take as long as you need. Weeks. Months. I'm marrying you forever. I can wait.' That gave me the freedom to decide what I wanted or didn't want. I was completely in charge. No guilt whatsoever."

## PERMISSION TO SAY NO

Part of our honesty about the past and how it affects our view of sex does include the word no. As victims, our "no" was not heeded, and most times, it was mocked or used as a signal for further violation. Because of that, we often believe we have no right to say no in marriage, particularly if we are women and we want to be submissive to our husbands. To say no equals disobedience.

In light of this, we forget the beauty of mutual submission, of loving each other so well that each of us can love each other's nos as well as yeses. Paul instructs in Ephesians 5:21: "And further, submit to one another out of reverence for Christ" (NLT). That verse often gets ignored, obscured by the wife-submitting-to-her-husband verse. But both verses are there. And we choose submission—not so that we lose ourselves and our identities or our power to say no. Instead, we choose to love the person we've covenanted in marriage with because we love Jesus. Out of our strong, deep affection for Jesus, we consider the needs of the other. Which also means, if you are freaked out, or a certain act triggers memories of your past abuse, your needs are valid. You are free, though it may be scary, to share that with your spouse so he/she has the opportunity to submit to you because of his/her love for Jesus.

## SEX IN MARRIAGE

Mutually gratifying sex is not a power struggle. It's not one person getting her way at the expense of the other. It's not one person's gratification over another's exploitation. If it has become that for you, it may be wise to invoke 1 Corinthians 7:3–6. Read these verses prayerfully, together.

> "The husband should fulfill his wife's sexual needs, and the wife should fulfill her husband's needs. The wife gives authority over her body to her husband, and the husband gives authority over his body to his wife. Do not deprive each other of sexual relations, unless you both agree to refrain from sexual intimacy for a limited time so you can give yourselves more completely to prayer. Afterward, you should come together again so that Satan won't be able to tempt you because of your lack of self-control. I say this as a concession, not as a command" (NLT).

Note that this is not a commandment, but a guideline. If you are married, you have given your heart, mind, soul, emotions and body for another—to have and to hold until death parts you. Which is why having an affair is an affront. By doing so, you have ripped yourself away from your betrothed and joined another person, outside of covenantal relationship.

If you are both struggling in the sexual arena, a mutually agreed upon timeout may be in order. Not to hide. Not to grow in bitterness. Not to breathe a sigh of relief. But to pray. To seek God for healing. To ask God to work in the broken parts of you. To get counseling. To take responsibility for your healing. To re-examine your marital commitment. For your spouse, this may be a time of reflection as well, considering what he/she has done to trigger your responses, or how demanding sex has made you feel used. You may both agree to therapy together.

## I'LL JUST NEVER HAVE SEX

Some folks have read these verses and chosen deliberately to never have sex again—for years. Sex has become a reminder of far too many painful things, so instead of dealing with that pain in a healthy manner, they've chosen to eliminate the trigger altogether. This, then, deeply damages their marriage, how their spouse feels about herself/himself, and gives Satan a chance to wreak havoc however he sees fit. Some sexless spouses resort to pornography, illicit affairs, emotional affairs, complete emotional shutdown, or erratic sinful behavior. In one case I know of, the spouse was so overwhelmed with past issues that instead of healing, she left her family. She preferred the devastation of divorce to dealing with her past issues. The aftermath of that meant devastation both to her children and to her grieving spouse, who desperately wanted to work on the situation with her.

Please hear me. I am not advocating submission to an abusive, controlling spouse. I'm not saying you have to put up with demeaning behavior. You, after all, are also loved by your Creator and are worthy of being loved, cherished and cared for. But there does come a reckoning in every marriage for the sexually abused person, a crossroads where we make a deliberate choice to either heal or give up.

Please don't give up.

Light awaits at the other end of the tunnel.

There were so many times I felt like abandoning my battle to enjoy and understand the beauty of sex. I felt like it was entirely, utterly unfair that I married a man whose love language was physical touch. Why oh why would God do that to me? Why was my weakness the very thing my spouse needed from me, the thing I felt I couldn't give? Was God a cosmic jokester, putting people together willy-nilly just to see sparks fly?

There were times I couldn't fathom change, times I harbored resentment for my husband's need that seemed impossible for me to fill. Eventually, I learned I had to separate his needs from the situation and simply go to Jesus. Instead of complicating my very cluttered mind with what I felt Patrick needed or wanted, I simply switched my attention to Jesus ("out of reverence for Christ"), and asked Him to show me the next step. In that circle of two, a broken girl and the Almighty God, I regained some footing. I could do the next thing Jesus asked. I could choose to obey Him. I would make a choice to hug my husband, to kiss him, for the sake of the One who embraced me first. For His sake, I could make a choice for Patrick's sake. More often than not, my emotions and will followed my obedience.

## THE CHOICE

This ambivalence toward sex reminds me of motherhood. I am not a naturally nurturing mom. Perhaps because it hadn't been modeled to me, or perhaps because I don't seem to have motherly DNA. I don't gravitate toward bending low toward my kids and kissing boo-boos. However, like any other children, my kids fell down, hurt themselves, and needed me to love them through their injuries. I knew they wanted a connected, loving mother. So I asked Jesus for strength. I begged for help, actually. And the first few months of practicing nurturing felt robotic and strange. If a child came to me distraught and needy, I would say to myself, "Self, you need to bend low, scoop that child up, hug her, and love her. Kiss her forehead. Pray for the pain." I, who tend to be the poster child for authenticity, felt this exercise smacked of unreality. But eventually, I became a nurturing mommy. I won't be the poster child for Mother of the Year in this area, but I am much different than I was. Why? Because I chose to seek what God would have me do and then obey. I made a deliberate decision that I didn't want my children growing up with an un-nurturing mother. My affection and tenderheartedness followed my obedience.

It's been the same with my marriage. When I've made deliberate choices about sex, sometimes feeling rote and robotic, I've found that my feelings follow my choices. These choices are not coerced. I make them freely because I don't want to be a wife who is sexually distant from her husband. Granted, I fall in this area a lot. I frustrate my husband. I send mixed signals. I hurt and reject him. I wish I didn't. But I'm much further along than I would have been had I not started making tough daily decisions.

## HOW MARRIAGE CAN HELP HEALING

Another thing I've learned is that I wouldn't be as whole as I am today without the backdrop of sex. Without my husband's desire to hold me, to love me, to cherish me, I wouldn't have had to deal with the times I'd been exploited in the past. I could've shoved those memories, and my resulting dysfunction, into a closet in my mind, living my life without any reminders. With the tenet of control at my disposal, I could arrange my life in such a way that I could keep my closet locked, never having to deal with the past.

I have hated this journey at times. But I have loved it too. Because I've become whole. Instead of viewing sex as that terrible impossibility, the presence of it has helped me wrestle (not always well) with my ambiguous feelings about it. I am learning to see it as a gift, a pathway to putting the devastation of my childhood behind me, and becoming a fully alive, invigorated wife in the present.

## MEN AND WOMEN ARE DIFFERENT

If we're going to be honest about our struggle with sex with our spouses, we have to also be honest about the physiology of each other as well. Men and women, though equal in the sight of God, are wired differently when it comes to sex. Psychologist Dr. Rosemary Basson of the University of British Columbia has conducted extensive research on how men and women approach sex.[23] Nearly one third of women never have desire for sex prior to the act. Those of us who are female abuse victims often feel like we're supposed to have desire, and feel guilty for not having it. But maybe that's more of an indication of biology than damage. Maybe it's a little more universal than we once thought. What would it look like if we offered ourselves grace in this area? For a woman, the sexual act is more about connection and emotional closeness, and less about sexual release, which is why we tend to feel used and violated if the emotional part of us isn't wooed. Desire, for women, comes slowly and in the midst of the act. For men, it's typically prior to the act.

The kind of sex that helps both men and women have a connected, desire-filled sex life is one of mutual kindness. According to a *Psychology Today* article, "The type of sex that fuels desire is leisurely, playful, sensual lovemaking based on whole-body massage that includes the genitals but is not limited to them. This is the lovestyle that many surveys show women prefer, but often don't get. One of women's main sexual complaints is that men are non-sensual—too rushed, and too focused on the breasts, genitals, and a quick plunge into intercourse. Given Basson's view of women's desire, this complaint makes perfect sense. Rushed lovemaking doesn't give women the time many need to become aroused enough to experience desire."[24]

Whether we've been sexually abused or not, the implication is that for sex to be amazing, it doesn't merely involve the final consummation. It means listening, slowing down, playing, and enjoying each other. Researchers have found that men with erectile dysfunction fare just as beautifully in this type of sexual experience as do women who have ambivalence about sex.

Which brings us back to the title of this chapter. Honesty. Can you dare to be honest about all of this? Will you share this chapter with your spouse as a means to open up dialog about the marriage act? Are you able to share the deepest part of you, the scary parts, the wounded parts, the broken parts? That level of intimacy is rare, but beautiful. It's taken Patrick and me years to get to this better place. Lots of misunderstanding, stewing, withholding, regretting, and worrying stayed within us. When we dared talk about it, we began to grow in understanding for each other. Even today, in the light of high noon, I shared with Patrick about this chapter. Talking about the *Psychology Today* article still wasn't easy for me. But it was necessary.

I am grateful we've chosen to talk. I'm thankful our sexual relationship is sweeter, more vibrant, and mutually fulfilling now. But that didn't come by happenstance. It's a result of hard work, of gut-honest sharing, and the grace of God for both of us. I pray that for you, too.

## HONESTY WITH GOD

Honesty with our spouses or loved ones is an important part of the healing journey. Have you considered honestly asking God questions about your abuse? I've certainly asked plenty.

When I met Jesus, I happily dismissed those questions, preferring to simply believe God knew best, and my questions would be answered in eternity. Oddly, the more I heal, the more I allow myself the pesky ambiguity of questions. I roll them around in my mind, pray about them, ask others for their insights. I used to think that the hallmark of a completed healing would be the satisfactory answer to all my questions. Instead, as I walk in healing, I'm sometimes more confused.

- Why would a loving God, who is supposed to be a heavenly Father, stand by and watch me be raped?
- Why would a powerful, strong God not use His might to rescue all the children who have been victimized?
- Why would God expect the very hardest thing from me (sex) in marriage when it serves as a reminder of the abuse?
- Why did I have to endure what I did? Would I be a more stable, capable adult had I not walked through the devastation?
- Why did my pleas for help, even though I didn't yet know God, go unanswered?

- While I know that in heaven, everything will be righted, and I'll be fully healed, why can't I see more healing and justice this side of eternity?
- What kind of plan does God have for those boys who molested me?
- Why did God put me on this earth?
- If I fancy myself a loving parent, and I would've rescued my child from a predator, what does that make God?
- Why are those submission verses in the New Testament, particularly when women get exploited, and men use them as justification to abuse?
- Where was God when I was being assaulted? Aloof? Detached? There, but choosing not to rescue?
- Why can't God remove sexual desire from people who perpetrate? Wouldn't that make life easier both for perpetrators and potential victims?
- Why can't healing be instantaneous, like we see often in Jesus's interactions with broken people? Blind to seeing. Deaf to hearing. Lame to walking. Why does emotional healing take so long?

In writing these out, I feel a bit Job-like, small and pea-brained, trying to understand the workings of an Almighty God whose mystery remains, particularly when it comes to the problem of pain and evil. I know the platitudes. I understand the doctrine of free will. But knowing theology still hasn't helped me wrestle these questions and come out satisfied. They remain unanswered the more I wrangle them. And even when

I try to tack cliché explanations to each one, I cannot escape the niggling that something is not right.

## YOU ARE NORMAL

I penned these honest questions to simply let you know that healing from sexual abuse and its aftermath doesn't always mean you will have satisfactory answers. If you still have questions, you are normal. And if you live in the tension of those questions, frustrated with the answers, it's okay. Having questions (or even giving yourself permission to ask them) is an indication that you're on the road to healing.

Attached to my questions is a long rope of anger. I am angry that I wasn't rescued. Angry that it seems Satan's biggest weapon at his disposal is sexual assault and warping the sexual experience. Angry that I am forty-six years old and still struggling with this part of my life. Angry that sexual abuse continues to happen, that children are exploited daily, and that many prefer to believe the perpetrators over those harmed. Angry, angry, angry.

And yet I don't want to be one of those people who walk around full of rage, always hollering about sexual abuse, maybe directing my anger at men for the rest of my life. What benefit is it for me, or even for society, if I stay in that constant state of wrath?

## CONSIDER JESUS

In times like these, I have to stop and simply remember Jesus. Though (as far as we know according to Scripture)

He wasn't sexually assaulted, He did know what it was like to be exposed. He absolutely felt the weight of each sexual exploitation when He died for all sins on the cross. I wonder if every awful act flashed through Him as He hung naked and bleeding?

I think about how He treated the broken. How He had mercy on the woman caught in adultery. On the woman with the issue of blood. On the leprous man. On the woman at the well. All outcasted. Perhaps some of them shared our story. Perhaps they knew all too well the questions we ask. How did Jesus treat these folks? With compassion and an open embrace.

And then I think of Jesus washing the feet of Judas. It fascinates and frustrates me, until I realize I'm Judas. In focusing on all these questions, I act as if I am only a victim, only the recipient of sin. I forget that I hurt people too. I sin against others. I betray Jesus by the way I sometimes live. Yet He stoops to wash Judas's dusty feet. He washes my feet with His tears. And I'm undone.

Me with all my honest questions. You with all your honest questions. (See Bonus Chapter One for my responses to some common questions). Neither scares Jesus away. Even our sin doesn't remove Him from us. Our rage, either.

The questions I wrote (and think) will most likely haunt me until I breathe my last. The anger I have, I pray, will lessen with the wisdom of years. But no matter how much I question or direct my anger heavenward,

I am stunned to silence when I think of Jesus—He who represents the Godhead, He who shouldered what those boys did to me, and what I did to Him. I can live in the tension of those questions when I temporarily rest them in the arms of Jesus.

Honesty is hard, folks. It's excruciating to talk about sex openly. It's scary to voice the questions you've held inside about God and justice and sexual abuse. But keeping our fear of sex and our possible anger toward God bottled up eventually causes explosions and implosions—a histrionic reaction to the ones we love, and a deterioration of our faith. I give you permission today to honestly share your worries, traumas, fear, and questions with those you love and the God you serve.

## FROM PATRICK:

Because of Mary's ministry and vocation as a writer, she has often shared her story in different ways and in different settings. She wrote an article about this topic for a magazine that has now expanded into this book. The magazine asked if I would write a few paragraphs giving my perspective as the spouse of an abuse victim. I was surprised how many people responded to the article and particularly the little bit that I added. The question I got most of all was, "How do you handle not having the intimacy and sex with your wife that you should be having?"

This is a loaded question of course. It presumes a lot of things, such as the expectations one has of one's spouse when they get married and what is the appropriate amount of intimacy and sex in a marriage. It also presumes that I am "handling it" well. The truth is, if I were in the situation where my wife did not have any desire for me or desire for sex at all, I would not handle that very well. I believe intimacy and sex are a crucial component of marriage, and if they are completely absent, a case could be made that it is not a true biblical marriage. If my wife showed no desire to be healed and no desire to have a full and satisfying marriage with me I don't think we would still be married.

Mary's desire for healing is one of the reasons why I am able to persevere when things are difficult. When I see her wanting to follow God's will, it carries a lot of credibility with me. It doesn't mean that she has to perform and achieve; what it means is she wants to want to. Her brokenness and frailty in this area provides me an opportunity to be gentle, kind, patient, and self-controlled, which just happen to be fruit of the Spirit.

I do not espouse to the idea that men are driven sexually beyond their ability to control it. It may feel like that at times, but Scripture says otherwise. It says that when we are tempted, God always provides a way out. It says that with the Spirit indwelling us we are empowered to control our base instincts. I don't consider myself a super-Christian or holier-than-thou. But I do believe that if your spouse is willing to heal, and is turning to God for healing, that you have the resources to be the spouse he/she needs to help overcome the pain and wounds of abuse.

# CHAPTER
# 9

# PRACTICE FORGIVENESS

## DISCOVER THE ANTIDOTE TO BITTERNESS, THE BEGINNING OF JOY

*"Jesus said, 'Father, forgive them,*
*for they don't know what they are doing.'"*

LUKE 23:34, NLT

The song "Canon & Gigue in D" by Pachelbel plays on my computer as I type this. It had been one of my father's favorite pieces, and I walked the wedding aisle to its cadence. So much of that music makes me cry, a symphony of what was, of what has become of me in the aftermath of sexual abuse. There's a lilting hope in the strings as the piece finishes, but its start is dark, thrumming, almost depressing.

Forgiveness is the bridge between the low notes and the crescendo. It's one of the most painful, bewildering works I've accomplished. I used to think forgiveness was a one-time decision, like you chose to forgive Uncle So-and-So for his leering gaze on Tuesday March third, and from that point onward, you'd look at the man with kind affection and a jaunting refrain of forgiveness singing through you.

Not so.

There is no "forgive and forget."

We forgive only to experience another trigger, another memory, another consequence that sparks in front of us, igniting our ire afresh. When the anger comes, we fight condemnation. Didn't I forgive? Then why this emotion?

Yes, forgiveness is a deliberate decision, but it's also an ongoing choice. Much like when Jesus saved us, yet we still have to daily walk out our salvation. It's a life-long journey, this audacious choice to forgive the seemingly unforgivable.

As I mentioned earlier, it has actually been harder for me to forgive the people who were supposed to protect me than it was to forgive those boys who stole from me so many years ago. As a parent who loves her children, I simply do not understand people who didn't protect. I can't seem to get over that. So my forgiveness for my relatives is sometimes an hour-to-hour breathing of forgiveness. Which is strange sometimes since one of my parents no longer walks in the land of the living.

We've heard that forgiveness is for our sake, and I believe that. I am a better person when I'm not walking bent by unforgiveness and bitterness. I make awful, spiteful decisions when I'm bitter. I either withdraw or lash out. Or my behavior turns toward risky. Or it becomes extreme inaction. Probably the best way to understand how I've processed forgiveness is to read the letter I wrote on my blog to the boys who molested me. Note that I don't gloss over the sin. I don't excuse it or say, "Ah shucks, you didn't mean to do that." No. I have not forgotten the devastation they wrought in my life, the vestiges of which I still deal with even as I type this. Forgiveness isn't glossing over or forgetting. Forgiveness is beautiful and powerful because I do remember.

## THE LETTER:

Dear Boys of the Last Name that Roils My Insides,

I am still angry.

What you did. Oh, what you did. Your choices dug scars the size of channels in my soul. You stole me. My innocence. My wide-eyed trust. My valiant view of life. My bravery. All kidnapped. In the aftermath of the sexual abuse, I hollowed. I believed lies about myself.

I am unworthy of being protected.

My self-worth = my sexuality, but in the most warped way.

Did you think of these things while you satisfied your base desires? Did you realize you'd destroy a little girl's kindergarten life? Had you no shame to violate a five-year-old girl for your pleasure? You had so much bravery in your sin, violating me while your mom cooked. No fear. And yet, your actions made me run scared most of my life, always looking around corners, running, running, running, afraid a villain would grab me. You marked me. Ever since your violating act, a mark danced on my forehead for all abusers and violators to see, as if they were black light, and the mark fluorescent. It was a ticket for further predators.

I am still angry. I was so small when you took me into the woods. So incapable of running away. And if I had tried, your hissed words would make me turn around and be re-violated. "We will kill your parents if you tell anyone." To protect my parents, I kept my mouth shut tight. And I dared not run.

But if I stay camped in the land of vengeance my joy will emaciate. You will have won the conquest.

I met Jesus when I was fifteen years old, ten years after you scared the hell out of me, five years after my father died. Gentle Jesus found me just in time. Those suicide swirling thoughts had hyper-charged my mind. I wondered what in the world I was doing here on this green, green, tall-treed earth. Was my purpose to be violated? To be used by others like you two? Or did I have some other unknown purpose?

Under an evergreen tree, the memories of your violation stung my eyes. And yet there, in that sacred place, I met Jesus. He took my sin (oh so many sins, innumerable were/are they) and flung it eastward in a projectile billions of miles away from me. He cleaned me, scrubbed my aching heart, and started me down the painful/beautiful road of healing. He took on my sin and my pain.

He changed my "I was" statements into "I am" statements.

I was molested. I am cherished by God.

I was stolen from. I am given everlasting, joyful, abundant life.

I was less than. I am more than I ever thought I'd be.

I am now free to forgive you. I am free to look upon you with grace-graced eyes. I am made whole by a holy God. Alleluia!

I understand better now. I thank God that by the time I reached your age, I met Jesus. I could've been you. I could've given in to the vile urges inside, crossed over many a barrier, had I not been rescued. Without Jesus, I shudder to think of what I would've become. Which brings me to a vulnerable place, and a deep, deep sadness for you.

If statistics play out, you didn't violate me for kicks. You did what had been done to you. You imitated the life you had. You acted out on the very thing that agonized you. The thing you hated is what you became. There came a day when you made a choice to give in to the madness in your head, where you believed you deserved satisfaction. Someone stole from you, so you may as well steal from someone else.

I see Jesus, naked on the cross with labored breathing. He understands the vulnerability of nakedness. On that cross He could've crucified all the violators, all those who sent Him there, but He breathed wild forgiveness. He chose to do what you did not. He suffered for someone else's sin. And instead of enacting vengeance, He ushered in an era of grace.

I wish this Jesus for you.

I worry about you. Maybe you've stuffed your memories of the little community near the salty water. Maybe you've scrubbed those woods from your mind. You've shoved it way, way down. Guilt riddles you, but you cannot articulate why. I'm proof, beautiful proof, that you can be set free. You can be scrubbed clean. You can be forgiven.

But you cannot heal in silence. An untold story never heals. I challenge you, as that scab-kneed girl you sexually assaulted, to give it up. Tell the story. Ask Jesus to forgive you.

All I can do is pray you'll find this letter through some beautiful God-breathed serendipity and finally want to be set free from what you did to me. I forgive you both, you brothers in crime. You brothers who ruined one year of my scared and scarred life. You brothers who most likely were violated too. Come to the fount of forgiveness, inaugurated by Jesus. Let my words serve as your entryway:

I forgive you.

My mountain of sins toward a holy God dwarfs the molehills you enacted against me. I read Jesus's words about the unmerciful servant and understand: "Then the king called in the man he had forgiven and said, 'You evil servant! I forgave you that tremendous debt because you pleaded with me. Shouldn't you have mercy on your fellow servant, just as I had mercy on you?'" (Matthew 18:32–33, NLT).

If I really, really believe in naked Jesus on the cross who bore all my shame and sin and muck, then I have to believe His sacrifice is sufficient for you too. His mercy sparks deep mercy in me toward you.

It's odd this affection, this ache I have for you two. I long to see you free from those memories, from the abuse you enacted and the abuse you faced. I can't offer clever solutions or pay for years of therapy to eradicate the pain. All I have is beautiful Jesus. All I have is my life made whole. All I have is my testimony. All I have is this: I am okay. I am wildly loved by my Creator. I am healed. I am living a life of truly impossible joy.

I am angry. But the anger redirects when I realize that Satan's greatest weapon is sexual violation. I'm angry at the powers of darkness that ignite deep, awful, scary soul wounds through pornography, sex

MARY DEMUTH

trafficking, sexual abuse, and sexual addiction. I'm flat out rage-filled because he has succeeded in stealing, killing, and destroying so many lives.

This must stop. For my sake. For your sake. For our sakes.

Satan, you cannot have these boys now turned men. Satan, you are not allowed victory in this arena. Jesus trumps your vile deeds. What you gleefully applauded in the darkness, Jesus heals audaciously in the light. You cannot and will not win. Light always, always, always pushes out darkness. Always. Your days are numbered, and those who follow Jesus are sick to death of your sexual schemes against humanity.

We stand for healing. We stand in Jesus's strength for the sake of future radically saved lives. We who know redemption are tired of miring ourselves in the painful past. Instead we will stand. We will dance. We will give our healed lives to rescue souls from the darkness. What Satan intended (and even you, brothers) meant for evil, God makes a holy turnaround. We who desperately needed rescue are now agents of rescue, of reconciliation, of forgiveness.

Oh that you would experience this new, new life Jesus offers you, brothers of the last name. I invite you on the journey. And if we ever meet under the evergreens, by God's life-altering grace, I will hug you. I will pray for you. I will weep. I will say forgiveness words. I will welcome you to the family of the messy-yet-redeemed.

> Standing in the glorious, sweet light of Jesus,
> Mary, no longer five, wholly loved

As a Jesus follower, forgiveness has to be a part of my story. Because I have often offended a holy God, I have such a great need for His forgiveness. Often my responses to abuse and pain have been sinful. It's sometimes easier for me to point to everyone else's sins against me than to honestly look at how my responses have been sinful too. In light of that, sin abounds, and the need for forgiveness rises. I've been forgiven much, and since I have, I must extend that same gift to others who have hurt me.

I pray this letter helps you process how you've felt about those who have exploited you. Perhaps writing a letter like this will be a part of your healing journey. You don't even need to send it, blog it, or read it on video as I did. But getting out all those angry emotions, that feeling of helplessness, and turning again toward Jesus in the midst of your recollection, may help you find healing.

## A FORGIVENESS TOOL

Another tool you may want to consider is an acronym developed by Everett Worthington Junior. I discovered it in *As We Forgive* by Catherine Claire Larson.[25]

To forgive, we must REACH.

**Recall the hurt.**

Don't deny or minimize the pain or memory. Forgiveness, as I mentioned before, is not forgetting. It's remembering the pain, then making a choice to forgive anyway. That's what makes forgiveness powerful and difficult. We can't forgive what we've stuffed. We must open the wound, own it, and admit that it hurt like crazy.

**Empathize with the person who hurt you.**

In other words, try to see the trauma from the other person's perspective. This is not easy. I learned to do this, as you saw above in my letter, with the boys who molested me, remembering that they who victimized most likely were victims themselves. Hurt people hurt people, the cliché goes, but it's true. Finding a way to jump into the shoes of the offender is important. It helps you see them not as monsters but as human beings.

**Altruistic gift of forgiveness.**

To offer this gift of forgiveness, it helps to have an anchor—a keen memory of a time when someone graciously forgave you. Remembering this altruistic gift helps us to know how to offer it. If you can't recall a time when someone outrageously forgave, consider Jesus's amazing forgiveness of you.

**Commit publicly to forgive.**

It's one thing to write forgiveness words in your journal. It's another to share your desire to forgive with a close friend. Determine to forgive, but tell someone else about it. That kind of accountability helps you when you don't feel like forgiveness. Once your desire is "out there," you're committed.

**Hold on to forgiveness.**

This is the hardest for me. I choose to forgive, but then I do take-backs. Or the emotion of the situation attacks me again. Or another infraction blares into my life. It takes tenacity and grit to continue to choose to forgive. It's not an emotion; it's a choice.

## THE GREAT REVERSAL

Many sexual abuse victims get stuck in their journey of healing even after they've forgiven the offender because awful memories surface, and they have to grit their way to further forgiveness. But there is still one more person they haven't forgiven: themselves. So many of us blame ourselves for unwanted sexual touch. We think we enticed, asked for it, deserved the leering gaze and touch somehow. We cannot conceive of the abuse without first thinking of what we did to cause the attention or bring on the abuse.

If this is your experience, I'd like you to read through REACH one more time, but instead of offering to forgive the abuser from the past, I'd like you to offer forgiveness to you in that moment. Although you most likely didn't do anything to contribute to someone else's sin, you still believe you did. You may battle monster-thoughts of unworthiness because of this. It's time to offer yourself the grace you so audaciously gave those offenders. It may help to walk through this exercise with a trusted friend or counselor.

## FORGIVENESS IS NOT ENABLING

One thing I don't want you to feel as you walk away from this book is that forgiveness equals enabling. In terms of those boys, the Statutes of Limitations have long run out, and I am not even entirely sure of their identity. There is no evidence other than my story. Thankfully, God sees all of our stories, and He will, on the streets of the great hereafter bring everything to light. His justice will be perfectly meted out.

But that doesn't mean we shouldn't work toward restoration here on earth. While it may not happen for me and these boys, there are hundreds of thousands of perpetrators walking free, able to molest again, because justice in our land has not been served. I hate it when I see our judicial system (or church system or school system) ignore the cries of victims, while preferring the perpetrators. For our sakes, we must forgive, but that doesn't mean we let go of punishing perpetrators.

If I had full knowledge of those boys-now-men's identities, I would do my best to see if they were still offending. If I could, I'd stop further abuse by reporting what I know. That's forgiveness plus justice. But since I can't prove their identities, I can pray. I can hope that God has taken hold of those men and changed them. And I can cling to my forgiveness of them, not as a token of my merit, but as an indication of the wild, outrageous grace of God in my own life.

When considering forgiveness, think on the kind of life you want to have. Remember the people you admire, those who seem to have that effervescent quality of life you have longed for. Chances are, they've learned the secret of forgiveness, of letting the past go to anticipate the now. Forgiveness is the bridge between the two halves of your life—then and now. The more you dwell back there in rage and bitterness, the more you are tied to the injury. Forgiveness helps you live blessedly present tense.

## FROM PATRICK:

Forgiveness was and is a crucial part of my story as well. At first, the anger and frustration I felt in my marriage was primarily directed at Mary for not living up to what I expected or wanted her to be. If I let my emotions fester in my head, they tend to migrate to my heart. I become resolved in my thoughts. I assign motives to Mary and convince myself that she will never change. Resolution and conviction are results of sin that has taken root in my life. When I stop viewing my wife—or my kids, or even strangers—the way Jesus views them, it is called sin. It erodes our relationship and if left to its own direction, will define the relationship.

So becoming a forgiver is an important part of Mary's and my healing process. I begin by saying (or praying), "Jesus, what am I not seeing or doing here? Why do I feel this way about Mary?"

And in His own way, He begins to reveal my own insecurities, my own false motives, my own frailties and failures—not to destroy me, but to restore me (the biggest difference I have found between the Holy Spirit's voice and the enemy's). I allow myself to be open to a new perspective on why the other acts the way she does. And if I can see, and feel what she sees and feels, it is called empathy.

Forgiveness on this level must have a significant degree of empathy to be lasting. If I can see that her response to me was triggered, I can offer grace, much like Jesus always offers grace to us. It becomes a natural extension of empathy to extend forgiveness, particularly to those who we love the most.

Easy? No.

Repetitive? More common than not.

Essential? Always.

To the boys who caused the triggers in Mary in the first place, I also must offer forgiveness. They were stupid, stupid kids. I can't identify with what they did, but as Mary has pointed out, they were most likely treated just as badly by someone in their lives. It doesn't excuse it by any means, but it is important to find empathy in some form or fashion.

In some ways it helped Mary to know how angry I was with the boys who did this to her. It validated her anger as well. It made her feel not so alone. I once shared with her what I would have done if I had stumbled upon those boys doing those things to her, that I would defend her no matter the cost to me. I think this helped her. But it was also important to walk the forgiveness road with her. Whereas I validate her pain, I must also validate that it is okay to not let it control her anymore.

# CHAPTER
# 10

# RETRAIN YOUR BRAIN

## CHANGE YOUR TODAY BY THINKING DIFFERENTLY

*"For, 'Who can know the LORD's thoughts? Who knows enough to teach him?'*

*But we understand these things, for we have the mind of Christ."*

I CORINTHIANS 2:16, NLT

Real change in moving from dysfunction to health comes through a rejuvenation of our minds. I've written a number of times about this subject in my Christian living books mainly because it's a titanic struggle for me. My mind is where I hide. It's where those flashbacks and nightmares live. It's where my desire or lack of desire for sex originates. It's the place where I berate myself for not being enough, not healing enough, not living abundantly enough. It's where those pornographic words and images remain cataloged, decades after my addiction. It's where my worthlessness (or my perception of it) reigns.

Just ask my husband; my mind is a scary place. Sometimes I let him in on what's going on in there, poor guy. Maybe the reason I'm a writer is so that I can regurgitate my angst and not pester others with details ad infinitum. It seems to me that those of us who have been abused can either have overactive imaginations and crazy-busy brain waves, or we shut down completely. I've been in both places, and, frankly, the numb brain scares me more. At least with the chaos I can attempt to train it. (Insert laugh track here).

## THE SCARY THOUGHTS

The problem with an abuse victim's mind is primarily the mean voices residing there. Some of mine relating to sexual abuse include:

- You are not worthy of protection.
- How creepy that you enjoyed sex last night.
- You'll never get over what happened to you when you were five.
- You'll probably never heal.
- Your abuse was no big deal in comparison to others. Why can't you just get over it?

- Because you're so "committed" to healing, you dredge it up and become worse. Shame on you.
- You are dirty, way down deep.
- You somehow welcomed your exploitation.
- Your worth is based on whether people use you. You're put here to be used.
- "Just okay" is the best you can hope for in this life.
- Joy is for other people who didn't grow up with your story.
- You are different, and not in a good way.
- Sex will never be fun or playful or connected.
- You'll continue to hurt your spouse in the sexual arena because you are selfish and self-absorbed.

Just typing that list reminds me again that I have a long road to journey when it comes to healing from all this mess. I'm learning that these kinds of mean voices are entirely and utterly counterproductive. They don't inaugurate change. No, they make shame grow monstrous, and shame never motivates. It only de-motivates.

## MEAN PEOPLE

I've learned through all this that I am my own mean girl. Perhaps you are too? Or your own mean boy? Do you yell at yourself in your head? Did some of my inner rantings resonate with you? There are things I've told myself I would never breathe to another person. I've berated myself, called myself lazy, ugly, a loser. I've despaired over this. Wondered why I did it. Puzzled over why it's a struggle.

Then I thought about mean folks in general. They usually victimize others because they have their own insecurity and injury. To cover up their vulnerability, they maim others with vicious words. It's a defense mechanism to keep people far away from their hearts.

How is this true for me? For you? Has your own insecurity and injury caused you to turn on yourself, call yourself horrid names in the aftermath of abuse?

Do you victimize your own vulnerability under the guise of trying to be self aware and godly?

Would you say that the inner voice that shames you is Jesus's voice?

How has injuring yourself kept you from your heart?

Have your mean words resulted in positive change? Freedom?

## CHAOS IS COMFORTING

Part of our battle with the mind is seeing that abuse is our comfortable, cozy place. I know this sounds odd. But honestly, when my life is going well, and no conflict invades, I get nervous. I know how to live with stress, but I cannot seem to live well with joy. So to keep in that comfort zone, I stay in my head, isolated with my abusive thoughts.

We must settle issues of personal worth because if we do, we'll stop running back to the "safe" place of abuse. We'll stop entertaining those awful thoughts against ourselves. It's time we stop being mean. It's time to be gentle and kind with ourselves.     O n e time I let my hubby know what kinds of words I pummeled myself with. After he heard how hard I was on myself, he said, "Mary, I would never treat you that way. And you wouldn't treat others that way. Why in the world would you treat yourself like that?"

Ask yourself this next time you're being mean to yourself: Would you treat your best friend this way? And if you did, what would he/she feel? What would those words do? Would those words motivate? Cheer? Or would they bring shame and condemnation?

## RETRAINING YOUR BRAIN

I've learned to retrain my brain. I'm not fully there yet (just read my list above), but I'm further along than I had been. I've done this by following the advice of my friend D'Ann. In love and steady kindness, she handed me a spiral bound set of 3x5 cards. "On one side of a card write the lie you've believed about yourself," she said. "And on the other, I want you to write a Scripture that debunks that lie." So I did. And I kept that little spiral reminder next to me in the nightstand drawer. Here's an example:

Lie: "God likes to abandon me."

Truth: Zephaniah 3:17 "For the LORD your God is living among you. He is a mighty savior. He will take delight in you with gladness. With his love, he will calm all your fears. He will rejoice over you with joyful songs" (NLT).

## PRESENT TENSE LIVING

Another thing I've done has been to move from past-tense words about myself to present-tense sentences. I alluded to this in my letter to the brothers who molested me, and I fully explored this practice in my book, *Everything: What You Give and What You Gain to Become Like Jesus.*[26] Here's an example:

Past tense: I was molested.

Present tense: I am cherished, nourished, and wildly loved by the Creator of the Universe.

As human beings, we are wired for story. If we leave our story open-ended, the mind has to continually re-think the story and mire itself there. Rewriting our stories in the present tense with a positive conclusion frees up that tangled part of our mind. It helps us to move on.

Seeing my identity, not through the lens of the past but through the power of the completed present tense, has helped me reframe who I am right now. It's helped me to retrain my mind to think of how God is working in my life right now. Present-tense living affirms one of my favorite verses:

Isaiah 43:16–21 (NLT):

> *I am the LORD, who opened a way through the waters,*
>
> *making a dry path through the sea.*

*I called forth the mighty army of Egypt*
*with all its chariots and horses.*
*I drew them beneath the waves, and they drowned,*
*their lives snuffed out like a smoldering candlewick.*
*"But forget all that—*
*it is nothing compared to what I am going to do.*
*For I am about to do something new.*
*See, I have already begun! Do you not see it?*
*I will make a pathway through the wilderness.*
*I will create rivers in the dry wasteland.*
*The wild animals in the fields will thank me,*
*the jackals and owls, too,*
*for giving them water in the desert.*
*Yes, I will make rivers in the dry wasteland*
*so my chosen people can be refreshed.*
*I have made Israel for myself,*
*and they will someday honor me before the whole*
*world.*

Take note that God had performed a great deliverance for Israel. He rescued them from certain peril, destroying their enemies and placing the Promised Land before them. And yet, God tells them to forget all that. As I write this book, I worry that I'm dredging up what God has settled. I am doing it for your sake, but it takes its toll. I'm in danger of remembering too much.

MARY DEMUTH

## AN EPIC TO ANTICIPATE

Pastor Mark Buchanan sat with a woman like me who had a similar story. After he heard it, he threw a desperate prayer heavenward, not knowing what to say. "And then God slipped me an insight, timely as manna dropped from the sky. He showed me that her past was beyond repair, at least on my watch. If there was any good thing there was to salvage, I knew not how. But in the same instant God showed me she still had her future. And it was vast, unbroken, pristine, radiant. Her past was a tragedy to lament. But her future was an epic to anticipate."[27] That's our story too. We cannot alter the past, but we have the power, through Jesus, to anticipate The Next.

Have you ever felt like sexual abuse is your exile? That it's set you in a place you'd rather not be? A place not of your choosing? A mindset that haunts you? God spoke to the Israelites in their exile, encouraging those exiles to change their thinking or they would miss the great things He planned to do. If we stay locked in the isolation of our minds, always rehashing the old story, preferring the place of exile, we will not be able to perceive or see the cool things God will do.

I am proof that God hews rivers in dry river-beds, pathways through thorny thickets. He does the impossible. I'm living a life of impossible joy right now because of the new things God has done. Had I coddled my thoughts of unworthiness and believed them

160

forever, I would not have seen God's great deliverance in the now.

Our past is something to lament. But our future is something to anticipate with joy. A future-oriented mindset sets us free from the shackles of the past. After all, we are much better motivated by the promise of something on the horizon, than the threat of something lurking behind. If a killer is chasing us, we flee, and then hide. We are not running in a direction toward health or healing; we're simply reacting to an enemy. If, however, a dream hovers before us, just out of our reach, we run with purpose toward it, longing to catch it. That sort of forward momentum changes the course of our lives. We move from erratic hiding to purposeful pursuit.

## OUR GREATER PURPOSE

The Isaiah verses hint at this purpose, ending with a beckoning to Israel to honor God before the entire world. That's the power of our stories. We have the potential to embrace this oft-memorized verse: "And so, dear brothers and sisters, I plead with you to give your bodies to God because of all he has done for you. Let them be a living and holy sacrifice—the kind he will find acceptable. This is truly the way to worship him. Don't copy the behavior and customs of this world, but let God transform you into a new person by changing the way you think. Then you will learn to know God's will for you, which is good and pleasing and perfect" (Romans 12:1–2, NLT).

Interesting that Paul uses the word "bodies," the very thing we struggle with as sexual abuse survivors. That we take what was abused and used and offer it as an offering, and as we do that, we allow God to change the way we think about ourselves, this world, and our relationships.

## FROM PATRICK:

Mary and I met in church, and our Christian faith was a central factor in our friendship and in our lives as we looked toward the future and what God wanted to do with us as a married couple. For me, being a believer in Christ is the foundation for how I approach our relationship. It means that I have to take His Word seriously, even when it means that it costs me my expectations of what my wife would be like after we were married.

I was, thankfully, never abused but that means it has been difficult for me to relate to her at times. If I have a problem I just compartmentalize it. It took me a long time to come to terms with the fact that a problem as serious as abuse cannot be crammed into a file in the back of your mind. At least not in a healthy way. I found myself giving her advice like, "Just don't think that way," which as it turns out, is not very helpful.

My journey with being married to an abuse victim is really a story about Jesus changing me to be more like Him. To hear her with His ears, to respond to her as He would respond, to love her as He would love her. He continues to change my heart in ways that are less selfish and demanding, to more empathetic and generous. Not an easy journey, but one I committed to Mary, to those who attended our wedding, and ultimately to God who brought us together.

# PART THREE

# LIVE A BETTER STORY

So many of you reading this book believed that you enticed your perpetrator to violate you. You look over the key moments of your life, the things you did or said, and fret to micromanage your memory, trying to figure out what you could have done differently. Let me say this:

It was not your fault.

You didn't entice.

You didn't ask to be hurt or violated or leered at or touched or abused.

The person or people who did those things to you were warped by sin, and they were wrong.

They wronged you.

You were wronged against.

Please rest there.

My hope in writing *Not Marked* is that you leave the book with tools to fully understand that and to continue your healing journey. But more than tools, I wish you wholeness—a place of joy and abundance that you may have felt eluded you all these years. Yes, you have a difficult past story, but my prayer is that your now story will shine with redemption.

# CHAPTER
## 11

# LIVE UNMARKED

## WHO YOU WERE IS NOT WHO YOU ARE

*"God has made me fruitful in the land of my affliction."*

GENESIS 41:52, ESV

I startle easily. Everyone in my family knows this (and sometimes exploit it by lurking around corners). On some level, I knew this was because of the sexual abuse I experienced, but I'm connecting the dots further. One of the most sacred parts of me, my sexuality, was stolen. And when it was stolen, it startled me. Shook me off kilter.

As a child I'd have terrible dreams where perpetrators would chase after me. I'd end up sprinting onto a pier, with nowhere to run but into the air and the water beyond. When I leaped up, a gunshot rang out, and I would awaken with a startle.

The dream symbolized how helpless I'd become—without rescue. I had nowhere to turn in the dream, and even when I jumped to save myself, someone shot me, and I started the process of death.

While I've been deeply healed, I think I'll always startle easily—perhaps a painful leftover from a traumatic past. How can that be hopeful? Maybe you're hollering at yourself for not getting over your own abuse. Maybe you're angry that you still do things that directly relate to the abuse that you wished you didn't do. Maybe you think no healing has taken place because you still have residual reactions.

Don't believe that lie. You are healing. And someday you'll be fully healed in heaven. The scars and startles are little leftovers to gently remind you that you're human, and that you all-the-more need Jesus.

## SHOULD OUR ENEMIES DEFINE US?

The last stanza of the song "Cedars of Lebanon" by U2 is instructive to those of us who live in the new aftermath. The gist of the lyrics are that we should choose our enemies wisely because they'll end up defining us, that those pesky enemies last longer than our friends will.

How much of my life has been defined by those two boys who stole from me at five? Have I given them far too much power? There was a large chunk of my life where they ruled my mind. Nightmares, daymares, flashbacks all tortured me for a time. And then as I healed, as Jesus took my hand and led me down a healthier path, the boys faded from memory. I can't remember their faces. I hope and pray they don't last longer than my friends.

But they will if I let them. If I stay back there in those bully memories for too long. Now I only visit them to proclaim healing, thankfully. But if I stay, they have a way of entangling my mind. I've experienced that in a marked way as I've written this book. Staying too tethered to those enemies gives them an opportunity to bite, to re-infect, to reinforce my perceived worthlessness issues.

God is in the business of creating new things. He places worth inside us simply because He created us. According to 2 Corinthians 5:17, God has new things for us. I fear that we miss those new things by staying too long with the bullies of former years. Let's not be so preoccupied with the past that we miss the power of right now, that we overlook a river through the desert of that memory.

Oswald Chambers says it beautifully. "Let the past sleep. But let it sleep on the bosom of Christ, and go out into the irresistible future with Him."[28]

We have an irresistible future! We don't need to follow U2's words. We don't need to be defined by our enemies. They do not have to have power over us. They cannot haunt us if we're pressing forward, looking to the future, awaiting the new things God brings.

## DO YOU WANT TO GET WELL?

Jesus asked the paralytic in John 5:6 the question He asks you today: When Jesus saw him lying there and learned that he had been in this condition for a long time, he asked him, "Do you want to get well?"

You have been in your condition many years now. Do you want to get well? Really? Would you rather rehash the past over and over in an endless loop of pain, or do you want healing? Or do you prefer to stuff it way down deep, becoming exhausted in the effort? I have found that most people don't pursue healing. The difference between the healed people and those still living in the past, defined by their enemies, is this: tenacious running after healing. You have to want to get well so bad it wakes you up at night.

I had an interesting conversation with a girl who had been sexually abused. We read John 9 together about the man born blind. I asked her why she thought Jesus spit on the ground, made mud, smeared it on the blind man's eyes, then asked him to wash in the pool of Siloam. "Maybe to see what he'd do next," she said. I thought about that, and the truth settled into me. I'd always puzzled over the spit and mud, but I hadn't thought about the action associated with it. Jesus could've easily healed that man with a word. But he chose to engage in the earth, spread it on his eyes, and ask him to do something about it. The Scripture doesn't say what would've happened had the man not obeyed and washed his eyes. But it does say the man obeyed Jesus, went to the pool, washed, and was healed.

## FOUR TRUTHS

Truth One: It is possible to be set free. You can experience the New in the Now. It's available, though the road toward health is often long and arduous. Every new territory gained is an opportunity to rejoice in what Jesus has done and an avenue to beckon others who hurt to join the journey. Each snippet of healing helps you become salve to those who are earlier in their healing path. The most satisfying times of my life, full of energized, effervescent joy, have been when I've had the privilege of coming alongside another and be a part of their healing story.

With Jesus, there is an irresistible future. It beckons. It allures. It hearkens. The past is gone, cradled by Jesus. Today is full of possibilities, and the future is clean and sparkling with potential. Oh to live that kind of freedom-infused, anticipatory life!

Truth Two: We are healed to become healers. Paul reminds us of this: "All praise to God, the Father of our Lord Jesus Christ. God is our merciful Father and the source of all comfort. He comforts us in all our troubles so that we can comfort others. When they are troubled, we will be able to give them the same comfort God has given us. For the more we suffer for Christ, the more God will shower us with his comfort through Christ" (2 Corinthians 1:3–5, NLT). We are made whole so we can usher in wholeness. We are set free so we can be agents of freedom on this enslaved earth. We are touched by Jesus so we can be His hands and feet and heart and life to others needing His touch. It's a great, sweet privilege, and the hidden gem of being healed from trauma.

Truth Three: There is no passive healing. We can't just lackadaisically want healing and hope it comes. Jesus touches us, yes, but He also asks us to do something. To pursue healing. To go to the pool and wash. To so want to be healed that you chase after it. "My eyes are ever toward the Lord, for He will pluck my feet out of the net" (Psalm 25:15, ESV). Note that the Psalmist makes a concerted effort to fix his eyes on God.

My friend Twilla, who battles a terrible cancer, is instructive. She has pursued physical healing tenaciously, exploring every option. And she's lived several years longer than she would have had she just given up and let the cancer overtake her. Of course this analogy breaks down because eventually she will die (and so will I, and you, and them). But the correlation remains: if you want healing, you have to pursue it.

Truth Four: Often you have to make difficult choices to completely separate from perpetrators so you can heal. Otherwise they open up a gaping wound that never heals, constantly re-injuring a raw sore. And even once you heal, there's no guarantee that you'll ever experience a safe relationship with an enemy. Even from a distance, they may haunt. But they don't need to have power over you anymore. You are a new person. You are a child of God. You are amazing, whole and restored in His sight.

## TIME TO LIVE A NEW UNMARKED STORY

Jim Loehr in his book *The Power of Story* wrote something I underlined and starred several times. "The most important story you will ever tell about yourself is the story you tell to yourself."[29] What story are you telling yourself? That you're an unregenerate victim of sexual abuse who will never feel whole or clean? That you'll always be marked, destined for further abuse? That you'll never enjoy a satisfying sex life? Have you resigned yourself to a lesser story? That kind of story only leaves room for your perpetrators, but it doesn't allow Jesus the space He needs to utterly redeem what they did to you.

Shauna Niequist had an aha-moment when she realized she'd been living a story based on hardship. "I realized all at once, sitting in church on a cold dark night, that the story I was telling was the wrong one—or at the very least, an incomplete one. I had been telling the story about how hard it was. That's not the whole story. The rest of the story is that I failed to live with hope and courage and lived instead in a long season of whining, self-indulgence, and fear. This is my confession."[30] It's my confession, too. I can't count the years I lived with a smaller story, content to resign myself to sadness and grief. Of course we must grieve. Of course we must be honest about our past. Of course we must master the art of writing lament psalms. Of course we must seek counsel. But there comes a point when living back there, wallowing in the pain, must end so our story of healing can begin.

Let's live on the soil of grace, tilling the decay underneath so that it can produce growth. When we live this way, we see our past as a gift—the very death that ushered us into Jesus's arms, the weakness that thwarted our self-reliance. It may sound strange, but I'm grateful for my story. It's supreme evidence of God's ability to transform a ragamuffin into a warrior, a wordless victim into a redemptive storyteller, a fearful slip of a girl into a brave encourager. I would not have the empathy I have for you had I not walked the path of pain. I certainly wouldn't have had the courage to write this book.

Just as God has a place in this world for me, He has a part for you to play in His redemptive kingdom—a you-shaped slot no one else can fill. You are strategically placed on this earth to be a breath of grace in other people's stories. Frederick Buechner affirms, "The grace of God means something like: Here is your life. You might never have been, but you are because the party wouldn't have been complete without you."[31] The world needs you blessedly alive, walking the healing journey, letting go of your "marked victim" story.

As I mentioned earlier, my husband Patrick once told me he wanted to see the last half of my life shine in comparison to the darkness of its first act. And I am shining in the second act. The story God has rewritten for me is about impossible joy and amazing abundance. The trauma of the past has faded—much like long-ago stretch marks or ancient scars. God has taken the violation of sexual abuse and reversed it.

I love what Psalm 90:15 promises. "Make us glad for as many days as you've afflicted us, and for as many years as we have seen evil" (ESV). Yes we experienced affliction. Yes we have seen evil. But God promises gladness in direct proportion to our sadness. It may not come all at once, but grace is in the sweet, sweet air.

Perhaps you've spent much of your life with an imprinted sexual abuse mark, a beacon inviting others to abuse you, a reminder to you and others that you carry secret shame. It seems so permanent, more indelible than a Sharpie pen's ink, as if the sexual abuse was pierced underneath your skin like a tattoo. I'd like to encourage you with a new story. Picture yourself walking down the street in your neighborhood with an "I was sexually abused" tattoo in blaring red ink on your forehead. People walk by, point at your mark. Some snicker. Others raise eyebrows. Some flirt. One person tries to stop you, asking for a kiss.

You rub your forehead in desperation, but the mark remains.

You take to watching your feet, sick of people looking at you and your mark.

You nearly run into Someone, spying sandaled feet on the sidewalk in front of you. You look up and catch the gaze of Love. Jesus weeps as He sees your mark. He wipes his tears, then takes his hand, still wet from tears, and washes away the mark. No evidence of the mark remains—it's been washed away.

You are now free to live unmarked.

Friend, live in that freedom!

# BENEDICTION

*May your life be marked by courage.*

*May your days be infused with grace.*

*May God send you many friends who bear your story.*

*May you heal in your sweet way.*

*May your prayers for healing find beautiful answers.*

*May you be a truth-teller in this secretive,*
*lie-addicted world.*

*May you be gutsy enough to live as a forgiving person.*

*May your mind be full of hope and peace.*

*And may you live a brand new story, unmarked, free.*

*Amen.*

# PART FOUR

# BONUS CHAPTERS
# AND APPENDIXES

Many people have asked me questions, so I've included them here—perhaps they mirror yours?—and my answers in the first bonus chapter. The second bonus chapter details an ancient, practical pathway to healing. Appendix One is an article I wrote about how to protect your kids from sexual abuse. Appendix Two is the blog post that instigated *Not Marked*, "The Sexy Wife I Can't Be."

# BONUS CHAPTER
# 1

# COMMON QUESTIONS ABOUT SEXUAL ABUSE

My expertise doesn't come from years of offering clinical counseling. These are simply my opinions after walking my own recovery journey.

**Do you feel disconnected after telling your story— as if it's not really your story? Is that good or bad? Do you feel better or more empowered after sharing it?**

Yes, there are times when I feel disconnected from my story, and if I really listened to myself talk, I might just cry. Sometimes it's good to work toward an emotional distance from your story. Thankfully, healing has helped me create that distance.

I don't know if I feel more empowered after sharing. Sometimes I feel depleted, actually, like a part of me has leaked out for others to consume. But I will say that the more I share my story, the more I marvel at God's grace. I'm stunned that I'm a functioning member of society with a great husband and three amazing kids. This is all God's grace.

**I don't understand how any good can possibly come from the sexual abuse I experience as a kid and as a teen. And when I share my story, I often wonder if those people have any idea how much I hurt.**

Oh I have felt your pain, and there are days I still remain in those same questions.

What good can come from suffering?

For part of that answer I go back to Job who lost everything—his children, his livelihood, his health, his will to live. He heard God at the beginning of his ordeal, but the scripture says he sees God at the end. That's what I want. To see God. Counterintuitively, I see God in the midst of my trials much more than I see Him in my prosperity. Those trials in my life drove me to God. Not finding appropriate love made me long for perfect love. Feeling alone helped me reach my hand to a God who was there. When I think about it that way, I begin to thank God for the trials because they plunge me back into His embrace.

Still, if I believe God is omnipotent, loving, and omnipresent, I have a hard time reconciling why He would allow a child to be abused. After all, as a parent, I would do anything to prevent abuse in my kids. So why wouldn't God? I don't have adequate answers even today. However, I've come to the place where I have chosen to rest in God's paradoxical plan. The truth is He will redeem it. How he accomplishes that is different for each person. Please know that these words I write are not flip or throwing out pat answers. These understandings have been hard won.

Do people have any idea how much you hurt? Probably not. Not everyone will understand your story. Not everyone will have empathy. And it's unfair to expect they will. Other victims may come close to understanding your pain. But the only One who truly understands exactly how you feel is God. So pour out your pain to him.

Mind if I pray for you?

*Lord, why? Why do You allow rape in people's lives like you do? Help us to wrestle long enough so that we nestle once again in Your arms. Be the protector we need. Help us to work through the questions. I pray they drive us closer to You, not further away. Lord Jesus, redeem these awful parts of our story. Make them sing. Use us to touch many, many women with Your grace. But we need to be filled with Your grace first. Fill us to overflowing. Right now. In this moment. Shower us with Your unconditional love. Help us see ourselves as You see us: spotless, beautiful, worthy of redemption. Amen.*

## I don't understand why sex could possibly be considered good. It only makes me feel used. What's your take?

I have to go back to the book of Genesis to see how sex was intended to be very good. Unfortunately, after the fall of humanity, even the most intimate act became tainted with power struggles, abuse, and all sorts of darkness. To be honest, I still struggle understanding the benefit of sex outside of procreation. But as I grow in my marriage, in that mutually beneficial place of surrender, I am beginning to glimpse its beauty. Sex is fun. Sex brings me closer to my husband in a way nothing else does, binding me completely to him. Sex means pleasure. It provides release, particularly from stress. It helps us take our minds off a crazy day. It teaches us servanthood and kindness. It can even be funny.

That being said, I don't think only sexual abuse victims struggle with sex being beautiful. In our subculture, we've been taught it's a dirty no-no for so many years, that turning that switch from taboo to terrific isn't easy.

So many people feel as you do, that sex isn't good, that it's an act where one person takes and the other gives more than she wants. Feeling used is very normal for a sexual abuse victim, and the shift from used to tolerable to enjoyable takes a lot of time. Part of that is re-training your mind that God creates good things—sex included. It's recognizing that you experienced violation, and that violation warped sex for you. Pursuing healing and daring to go to the dark places eventually brings light to sex's beauty.

## Is there forgiveness for me if I sexually abused another person?

Yes, there is. If it is at all possible to express your remorse somehow and ask forgiveness, you will experience that forgiveness even more keenly. Though this is not an easy thing to do, and some circumstances might dictate you not share, taking your secrets into the light will bring freedom.

The hardest person to seek forgiveness for (besides the victim and God) will be yourself. You know what violation is, and yet you did the very thing you hated to another person. Remember to offer yourself grace, knowing that without Jesus, we tend to duplicate what is knowable to us.

You don't have to carry the guilt any more. Make restitution if possible, but then choose to believe that Jesus died for sexual sin just as much as He died for gossip and murder and idolatry. Your sin is not unforgivable. To think it is, is to elevate your sense of justice over God's. He has chosen to forgive You by nailing your sin to Jesus on the cross. Quit grabbing it off the cross and hitting yourself over the head with it.

## But if I tell what happened to me, I will upset the dynamic of my family and break people's hearts and reputations!

That's true. You might. But no one ever heals in silence. And it is not shameful to tell the truth. You don't have to be punitive as you share it, hollering and yelling. Simply say what happened, how it made you feel, that you've chosen to forgive, and that you hope the people involved (either those who perpetrated or those who stood by) will find counsel and healing. You are not responsible for their reactions or words.

## What if I've told my story but I'm not believed?

That's okay. Your story is your story. Find someone else to tell who will hear you, pray for you, and validate the pain of what went on. If a perpetrator or bystander chooses not to believe you, that is their problem. Most likely, they simply can't deal with what they've done and are living under a mountain of shame. When you share, be sure you express grace, but if they don't believe you and call you a liar, it may be time to separate from that caustic person for a while, for the sake of your healing.

## What if my sexually abusive past was in part to blame for some awful sexual choices I made later?

Sexual abuse plays a huge role in the kinds of decisions we make, particularly in adolescence. Some folks freak out about sex and run from it (me) and others turn to promiscuity. Either response is a way to deal with the pain, by either avoiding it or reveling in it. To be set free from regret, share what you've done with a trusted person, and ask God to forgive you. Tell Him you're sorry. Acknowledge that what you chose to do caused self-destruction and pain. You will have consequences for your behavior, but that doesn't mean God hasn't forgiven you and given you a clean slate to move on from there.

**I can't read books about sexual abuse without re-living what I went through. It hurts too much. How do I heal if this is the case?**

Everyone has a different timetable in his healing journey. Learn to be kind to yourself. If books bring up things that are too difficult, put them down for a season. However, don't always give in to that fear, because there will come a time when you'll have to face what happened. Otherwise you will never heal.

**I've been told that my virginity is the most precious part of me, but I lost it through someone else violating me. So am I no longer precious?**

First, what happened to you was not your fault. Someone stole from you, violating your body and your trust, damaging your soul. You are not damaged goods.

God redeems even sexual abuse. He cleanses us. Your virginity isn't the most precious part of you; your soul is, the place where Jesus lives.

## Will I always struggle with this? I feel like it's so totally unfair.

Most likely you will always struggle on some level, but if you actively pursue healing, it will get better and better. I won't argue with you about unfairness because I agree. What happened to you was unfair.

## How can husbands of women who have experienced childhood sexual abuse be a supportive part of the healing process?

I'll answer this for any spouse, husband or wife, who wants to support their partner. First, I so appreciate your desire to help. Sexual abuse victims need community to heal, and being a safe spouse allows for that community. Obviously, expressing unconditional love and creating a safe place within the marriage provides a great foundation.

Beyond that, ask questions, but be sensitive to back off when you sense your spouse is shutting down. Reaffirm your love. Encourage counseling if he/she gets to a stuck place—and be willing to accompany your spouse if they ask. Praying for and with your spouse helps too. Being patient with their sexual fears, moving away from demanding, or taking their resistance personally, will help them find the space they need to heal.

**How do you move on from sexual abuse from both childhood and from a spouse? I wonder if it's possible to ever feel like a real person? I'm afraid I'll be just used for sex again. No one ever talks about sexual abuse in adult relationships, but it happens and happened in my marriage (11 years).**

After a recent talk about sexual abuse, a slip of a woman met my eyes, then started crying. "I just got out of an abusive relationship," she told me. "I had to get a restraining order." Her partner's abuse included demand for sex. Sexual abuse within adult relationships is a big issue, but as you noted in your question, very few talk about it.

My first encouragement is this: if you're currently in an abusive situation, find a safe place now. Time and distance will help you heal. If you were abused both as a child and an adult, I'd consider counseling to determine why you've continued in the pattern of being marked and attracting perpetrators.

I can only imagine the fear you must have in thinking about venturing back into the world of relationships and the potential of sex. Worrying that you'll simply be an object again is a very tangible fear. From my perspective, I can say that there are safe people out there, and any time you put yourself out there, you do take a risk. But you'll never meet the safe ones if you live in constant fear that they're all unsafe perpetrators.

## What is your response to people who say things like "That happened a long time ago. Why can't you just get over it?"

I'd ask a question back. When has someone you loved died? How long did it take you to "get over" that loss? Most of the time people who say that insensitive comment are either:

Completely oblivious to the trauma and devastation of sexual abuse, and are simply uncomfortable when you bring it up. This is their way of shutting you down.

Stressed that you brought it up because they have their own issues of abuse and are too afraid to admit to the pain.

Those who truly believe the sexual abuse causes no lasting damage.

Counselor Lucille Zimmerman asserts, "Sometimes Christians are quick to expect victims to heal in a hurry. Victims are preached at, given pat answers, and expected to forgive and forget. But just as Nehemiah had to acknowledge the extent of the damage before he could begin repairing the walls around Jerusalem, survivors need to take many long steps before they heal."[32]

Comments like these can derail you, make you feel very small, and push you further back on your journey of healing. When they happen, instead of seeing the comment as an indictment against you, see it as an indication of the other person's warped perspective. In other words, it's not about you; it's about them. Reframing their question in your mind will also help. Something like, They may think it's simple to get over sexual abuse, but they don't understand the process. I'm choosing today to be grateful at the amount of healing I've had. I'm further along than I was two years ago. I'm more resilient. I have more empathy for people. And I'm becoming healthier.

**I allowed myself to get overweight because I didn't want men finding me attractive. I still fear being a normal size. What can I do to gain strength and confidence? I need and want the weight off but I keep thinking men are going stare at me like an object.**

As I mentioned in the checklist in the Introduction, weight gain can be an indication of past sexual abuse for the very reason you stated. You fear being enticing. You fear unwanted advances. My gentle pushback is this: how will you deal with your issues if you create a hedge of weight protection around yourself? How will you grow? Heal?

That's why it's been excruciating, yet healing, to be in a marriage, having to face sex. Because I have to deal with it, I am forced to either give up or grow beyond.

There are other ways that are less health-damaging to protect yourself from perpetrators. Counseling will help you learn what kinds of people are predators, how to set appropriate boundaries, and what it means to live a freedom-infused life in the moment.

## How can I move from clothes of dark colors that cover me from my feet to my neck to keep me invisible in a world I don't trust?

See my comments on the overweight question above. When folks overly cover themselves, they are afraid—and they're avoiding dealing with the deeper issues. On the other hand, some sexual abuse victims resort to an opposite phenomenon, overexposure, where they show the world everything. Somewhere in the middle is the healthy place. We don't want to live our lives in terror about our own sexuality. But we also don't want to live in such a way that shows that all we are is a sexual object.

## How is it possible to completely let go of the abuse and learn to enjoy sex with your spouse? Like ever?

I'm not completely free of the effects of the abuse. Although I consider myself "not marked," the scars remain, and I have bad days when I don't enjoy sex. My main encouragement is to communicate openly about your stress about sex. Be articulate when it comes to your sexual needs, particularly what scares you and what blesses you. My husband truly wanted to know what triggered me to disassociate during sex because he loves me and wants us to have mutual joy during sex.

Be careful not to catastrophize your view of sex. When you think, *I will never enjoy sex. It will always be awful. I'll always have to tolerate it*, you shortchange the possibility of what could be.

If sex is physically painful, I'd encourage you to seek medical attention or possibly sex therapy. I'd also encourage you to share your story with your closest friend (as long as your spouse is okay with that kind of openness) and ask him/her to pray with you about this area of your life. Sometimes bringing the issue to light helps dissipate some of the darkness.

## Did you experience body memories or flashbacks? How did you deal with them?

Yes. Flashbacks happen—but not usually when I'm in the middle of sex. But body memories (when your body reacts to a particular touch and you don't exactly know why it does) come during sex. I'll recoil or shut down if I'm touched a particular way. That's why communication with my spouse is so important. For many years I didn't share these reactions with him. Instead I stuffed my recoiling, then playacted my way through sex. But now I'm learning to share, to be honest about what triggers my disconnection.

**One of many issues that came from childhood
sexual abuse is a deep sense of shame. It rears
its ugly head during intimate moments with my
spouse. How can I reassure my spouse that the
extended time and head-work it takes for me to
"go there" is not about desire or rejection of him?
And will I ever not struggle in this area? I heard
you talk once about how your husband knows he'll
never eat strawberries off your belly. That's me!
In a world that says that's part of "the fun," that
can be hard.**

That's a hard one because spouses do experience rejection when we're trying to conjure up a desire to have sex.
Doing that sounds like we don't "want" them because
we have to work at wanting them. The old cliché, "It's
not you; it's me" is true, but not wholly helpful when
you're explaining why it's hard for you.

Viewing marriage as a team instead of a he-she
need-meeting factory helps. It's not about you meeting
his needs, or him meeting your needs, but about both
of you meeting each others' needs. It's a win when both
of you are joyfully satisfied.

Working on your own issues is the gift you give
to your spouse, just as your spouse working on his/her
issues is a gift to you. You're in this together.

As to whether you'll ever get better, yes it is possible.
You will be more healthy next year and the year after as
long as you continue to doggedly pursue healing—not
only for your sake, but for your spouse's. There will be

times when you feel like giving up. You'll sometimes give in to the thinking that you'll never heal. You'll get discouraged. But remember, we all walk with a limp on this earth. None of us will be wholly healed this side of eternity. Your limp just happens to be sexual injury, which gets at the very core of you and touches on issues of identity and worth. It feels pervasive. When you get to that place of despair, recount how far you've come. And remind yourself that you will be fully healed one day.

As to the strawberries, I (still) can't imagine doing this, and I'm learning that that's okay. The measuring stick of my sexual relationship with my husband is not Hollywood. It's not even other Christians who share about their amazing sex lives or offer advice about how to be all that. The measuring stick exists deep within my marriage, a sacred place where we learn to love each other, sacrifice for the other, and express our love in us-shaped ways.

**How do I cope with the fact that I didn't want sex as a child? I wanted fatherly affection, but abuse from others seemed to be all I got. And now as an adult I still don't want sex, and I still desperately long for the fatherly affection that seems to have always eluded me. It's a struggle to say the least. I just want to hold someone's hand without having to worry that it will ever be more.**

Wanting fatherly affection is a normal need we all have. That you didn't receive it is something you'll need to explore and possibly work through in counseling. And that you did receive unwanted sexual touch convolutes your pain even further. I had those exact same feelings when I started dating. I wanted nothing more than to be hugged, maybe hold hands, but no kissing, certainly not anything else.

In light of that, I've also had to mourn the fact that I didn't receive what I needed from my father—and that I did look everywhere else for that kind of simple affection. I also looked for my mother's love in a similar way. In that journey, I've finally come to see that I'll have to grieve the loss of what I wanted as a child, and redirect my needs to Jesus. He is the only One who can truly fill me up. He is the only One who can meet that longing for an affectionate parent.

That being said, if you want to be married, sex will inevitably follow. It's something you'll need to work through now for the sake of your future spouse. Reading this book, seeing a counselor, asking for prayer, telling your story—all will help you on your journey toward sexual wholeness.

Another issue is the ick factor. When we've been sexually violated, it's inconceivable to see sex as beautiful. Making that switch from ick to wow! takes time.

That being said, sex isn't everything. Our culture tells us the opposite. You can have a fulfilling unmarried life without it.

**I feel like I'm living a lie by not talking about what I went through, but I'm afraid of how people will treat me if the truth came out. Why do I feel the need to hide when I wasn't the perpetrator?**

You are so very normal. Most sexual abuse victims feel extreme shame about what happened to them. They feel that if they tell someone, that person will judge them and think differently. And yet, as I consider my closest, sweetest friendships, I am drawn most to the people who tell me the muck, who dare to share the hard stuff. You will endear yourself to others (as long as they're safe) when you are honest. And you'll begin to find healing in the light of day.

**I believe that God can bring complete healing yet I have not experienced this with regard to the sexual abuse. I have forgiven and no longer have that in my heart (a long process with a lot of help from the Lord), but there are leftover issues that I deal with that seem so deeply ingrained that I am not sure I will ever be free from them.**

This is where community is helpful. You may not even know your residual issues, but people close to you will. Give your closest friends permission to tell you where you've allowed the pain from the past to influence your today. And be willing to see those issues as problems. Ask for prayer.

It sounds, though, that you are familiar with your issues. In this case, be careful not to dictate exactly how you want God to heal you. I've been guilty of seeing my problems and telling God to fix Issue A, only to realize He had something else He wanted me to address. Even give up control when it comes to the pace and manner in which you heal. God has this. He's big enough. He knows your issues more intimately than you do. Sometimes we simply need to rest our healing in His hands.

**My spouse takes it personally when I can't drum up the interest or desire. I so desperately want to be close, but resentment has built up on both sides.**

This is an extremely common problem, one that I experience frequently. What helps us is talking about our pain—Patrick sharing how he feels (rejection), and me sharing how hard it is to be healthy sexually. If we stuff our resentment, it gets ugly—then explodes. If you've gotten to the point that you can't talk about it, consider couple's therapy where you have a safe place to share your anxiety and sadness in the presence of a mediator.

**Do sexual abusers stop abusing children? If someone was abused by someone and never told and now the person who abused them has two children do they need to disclose the abuse?**

Yes, they can stop abusing.[33] But since sexual abuse is typically hidden, it's hard to know who will re-offend and who won't. (In other words, you can't tell by simply observing someone.) In terms of you disclosing the abuse, if the Statute of Limitations has not expired in your state, you have the choice to disclose the abuse and press charges. Keep in mind that the process for pressing charges and seeking justice can also be traumatic. As to the person having children, it's a really hard call. If you have a strong relationship and you see obvious symptoms of abuse, you can choose to bring that up to authorities.

## Is there a chance for Real Love after abuse?

Absolutely. I'm living proof—with twenty-three years of marriage to a man who still makes me laugh. I will say, though, that I had pursued healing prior to meeting him. One thing you can do for the sake of your future love is to tenaciously seek healing.

**Until recently, I never realized how much CSA (Childhood Sexual Abuse) had damaged the way I do relationships. I lack boundaries and I struggle when people let me down. Why do I expect perfect love from imperfect people? How can I stop equating relationship disappointments to how much I am or am not loved/cherished by others?**

Oh dear, you're treading upon my issues! I definitely relate to boundary problems (letting the wrong folks in, protecting my heart from the good people). I also equate rejection with worthlessness. My encouragement is to simply say you're a normal human being who has been wounded and needs healing—but that the healing will take time. The fact that you can articulate your issues indicates that a great deal of healing has already taken place. Be encouraged! Self-awareness is a great place to begin.

**What about the people who know they were sexually abused but don't remember details and thus can't "prove" it? I'm having a lot of problems with someone instrumental in my healing not getting it or understanding because I don't have the proof or specifics. I've shown him Patrick's video[34] but he says he can't relate because he doesn't understand how I don't remember and how he can believe it happened without naming the details. I'm despairing and so depressed.**

You are normal. I'd point your spouse to any number of articles on the Internet[35] or sexual abuse books. It's very common to suppress memories from a traumatic event. If your spouse can't see beyond that (he sees it as not logical to forget an event), the best thing you can do is find a counselor specializing in sexual abuse and pursue your healing that way, and pray that someday your spouse will understand what it is you're going through. I'm very sorry you're experiencing this.

**If someone knows beyond a shadow of a doubt that they were sexually abused but it has been buried**

**for over 30 years, and their life has some reflection that it has happened, do you think it is important to confront that person—who is now elderly and not very well? Should he work toward remembering what really happened? Is that really necessary for healing?**

I had an experience where I pressed for information about one of my own difficult memories with an elderly relative. The result was just a lot of pain and crying. I'd pray about the situation and see what kind of wisdom God will give you about your specific situation. That being said, I do believe you can heal without having to confront the person who perpetrated or who didn't protect.

Trying to remember is not an easy task, and may not be fruitful or productive. I have some black holes in my memory. I desperately want to know what fills the void. But I've come to the place where I realize God is sovereign and He is a gentleman healer. He will open this can of worms in His timing, or not at all. Rest your heart in knowing God will direct your healing journey.

**Since it's typically assumed (& true) that sexual abuse involves touch, how can one process no-touch-involved psychological sexual abuse? I imagine the principles for healing are parallel, but the nuances of differences can make it challenging from an application standpoint.**

Actually, one of the huge takeaways I found from Dan Allender's, *The Wounded Heart* was that whether the abuse was physical or not, the healing journey is similar. That's also true in terms of degree of abuse. What's difficult in your situation is that you don't have physical proof to show you were abused. However, hearing unwanted sexual talk, observing leering glances, being shown porn, and living in an over-sexualized environment are very damaging. You still feel like an object. You still feel used. You still feel shame. You still feel dirty. Don't minimize your process simply because you didn't experience "typical" sexual abuse.

**My question is how do you get over sexual abuse when a pastor held a gun at you using scriptures? Clergy sexual abuse is happening, yet many keep it silent.**

You get over it the same way others get over it—except that you have a difficult road of healing in terms of your relationship with God. I wish the church were a place of safety and protection. It should be.[36] But often it's not. Pastors, youth pastors, Christian spouses, priests are not immune to this sin. Like all sexual abusers, they use their power to demean and conquer, but they cloak that power using Christian words and threatening damnation if someone talks. Honestly, I think this is one of the hardest forms of sexual abuse to recover from because it skews the sacred.

I was shocked when I started uncovering widespread sexual abuse in closed religious communities like the Amish.[37] I ached when I read about a prominent local church covering up a sexual abuse scandal. The church has faltered. It should be a place of truth, light and honesty—but for many it's become the place where shame birthed and no one believed their story. Often churches demonize victims, tell them to keep things silent. It's wrong. And it causes many people to walk away from the very faith that could offer healing.

**I had so many abusers at all stages in my life— even some of the counselors I went to see (and they were supposed to be Christians). How do you learn to trust when this happens?**

I can't imagine how hard it must be to trust another Christian after such a violation. I did write a book about how to heal after others (particularly Christian leaders) hurt you.[38] Trust is earned, not granted. So when you venture into relationships again, be on the alert for truly trustworthy behavior. Trust your gut when someone makes you feel uncomfortable, and take tentative steps toward folks who act in trustworthy ways.

**I've been married 13 years. The first ten were pretty good, and then things fell off the rails. Part of that was my stuff, but part of it was having the reality of my wife's sexual abuse as an adolescent bubble to the surface. The scars of sexual abuse**

**directly affect attachment, intimacy, and sense of security—all things necessary for a healthy marriage. What can you share from your experience for the spouse of someone who was abused as a child? How can we help? What can we do to support healing? And how can we live in the interim when the scars of abuse actually get in the way of our relationship?**

First, read Patrick's words throughout the book. I believe they'll be a comfort and bring some wisdom to you as you navigate this journey.

It can be very difficult to become a victim of the fallout of someone else's abuse. As a spouse, it's all the more frustrating because you didn't cause the issue in the first place. You and your marriage are suffering for someone else's sin. Re-train your mind to consider Jesus in times like this. He, too, suffered for all our sin. There's a sweet kinship that comes when we realize Jesus understands.

On the practical side, allow your spouse to bring up the abuse whenever memories or emotions or thoughts arise. Don't sigh and give a resigned, "Okay." Listen without judgment or even comment about the abuser. Don't try to fix it (because you can't). Just listen carefully. Ask questions.

Offer to listen after a counseling session as the stories and emotions unspool even more.

And don't be afraid to ask, "What do you need from me right now?" Sometimes the need might be to be held through tears, sometimes it might be to stay away, or sit across the room and listen to rage exploding—again, without judgment. Be a safe place for your spouse to be on the healing path.

The best thing you can do for your own broken-heartedness about her abuse is to take your emotions to Jesus—particularly when she turns away from you, or can't seem to change at a pace that you'd prefer. I remember telling my husband about eight years ago, "I want to change. I want to be different. I just can't right now. There's some sort of blockage." I asked him to pray for me. I sought outside help. Eventually, the issue resolved, but not in fanfare or in one great moment. Over time, I began to desire my husband again.

What made my healing journey harder was when he gave in to his anger, saw my difficulty with sex as an affront to him. If I sensed this kind of anger, I wanted to withdraw even further because I felt like I'd never get over it, never be the wife he wanted, never get better. Bring your needs to Jesus, then reassure her that your love isn't conditional on her perfection or even desire in the marriage bed. That kind of grace opened me up to change and growth.

## How can the church better support people who have experienced sexual abuse?

First, the church leadership should undergo training to spot sexual abuse within their midst. They must create a written policy about how they'll handle an accusation of sexual abuse. And if a staff member or volunteer is accused of abuse, the authorities must be contacted, allowing the criminal justice system full reign to investigate. Churches should also share information with other churches, not silently shuffling abusers from one church to another.

Covering up abuse re-injures the victim in a very demeaning way. And blaming the victim for being abused also shatters him/her. Many churches have cultivated a culture of silence about abuse, furthering the shame. It's time for leaders and pastors to bravely share their own stories, to bring sexual abuse into the light. That kind of authentic, real community will create an environment where victims feel safe.

If you're despairing about the church's response to sexual abuse and predators, consider reading, "A Public Statement Concerning Sexual Abuse in the Church of Jesus Christ" at netgrace.org.[39] Many church leaders, including myself, have signed the document. They apologize for the way victims have been treated and outline healthy ways to deal with sexual abuse.

## At what point and how did you share your story with your children? How did they react?

I really worried about this. I didn't want to traumatize my kids, nor did I want to make them scared. I shared my story with each child as God opened the door. Each child heard the story at different times. I let their questions be my guiding principle. I only shared in response to what they asked, and I kept in mind where each child stood developmentally, spiritually, emotionally, and mentally. Now that my children are nearly adults, they all know my story. My son accompanied me on one of my keynotes where I shared my abuse. We had good interaction afterward.

I've seen how secrets can hurt a family. And having kept my secret for ten years, I know how lonely that can be. I want my kids to feel free to share everything with me, which also means I am willing to share my heart and life with them.

I also never shared details about the abuse with them. I recounted the story, much like I tell it to audiences. I don't believe sharing those kinds of details benefit anyone. And I'm also careful to remind them about healing—that I wouldn't be the person I am today without Jesus.

**What was the hardest step to get through: forgiveness or the memories of what happened to you?**

The memories have faded. They no longer haunt. But it's still a choice to forgive, even decades later. Forgiveness is hard.

**By the grace of God, I have not experienced sexual abuse. However, several of my friends have. I don't know how to ask good questions of them when they share their stories with me. I never want to be insensitive, but not being a survivor myself, it**

**seems I run that risk every time I ask a question. To a survivor, it might seem obvious how to talk about it with a friend—but it's not to me!**

It depends on the fragility of the person. If they are already sharing their story freely without breaking down, then asking questions actually dignifies their story. Even if they're breaking down, it's okay to ask questions. "What are you feeling? I want to understand. How can I help you through this? How can I support you?" As long as you're not asking to gain morbid information, and your intention is listening well and empathizing, go ahead and ask questions. You might want to preface your questions with one of these:

"Since I've never been in that situation, I want to understand how you feel. Would you mind if I ask questions?"

"You don't have to answer this, but I'm curious . . ."

"Forgive me if I ask something stupid or insensitive because I don't mean to . . ."

Also in the friendship be sure you're being vulnerable too. Sexual abuse victims sometimes stay in the victim role, and they can feel like they're the one with all the problems and their friends are all put together and fine. We all suffer on this earth. Suffer alongside and entrust your painful story with your friend too.

**How does a friend encourage a friend to seek help/ counseling in the recovery process, when it's obvious to everyone but the survivor that the abuse she**

**has suffered is affecting her daily life and hindering her relationships?**

This kind of conversation comes in the context of a very stable, grace-filled relationship, where the victim absolutely knows he/she is loved. Otherwise they'll see the suggestion as another nail in the coffin of their inability to heal. Pray before you have this conversation. Be humble as you approach it, not as an expert, or someone who is better than or knows it all. You might say, "I really love you. I want to see you healed and joy-filled, but I've noticed lately that you've been _____."
Then ask questions. If victims feel understood, and if they see the need for counseling on their own (because they discovered it by answering your questions), they will own their healing journey.

Keep in mind many sexual abuse victims want to heal, but the healing seems to come very slowly. Offer to accompany them to counseling. Send cards of encouragement. Pray for them. Affirm your love. Ask God to help you see the true need of your friend. There are times when He asks you to push back gently, to tell the truth when you see your friend believing lies. It might not feel good, but that kind of truth-telling love is necessary. Preface your words with, "You may not be able to see this in yourself, but I've been noticing _____." Or "As your friend who loves you and cares about you, I want to point out how your abuse is affecting you today. It will be hard, but I care."

**How do you have grace with people who, after hearing about your past, treat you like you're a fragile, traumatized person who is damaged beyond compare, even thought it's obvious in your life that the Lord has healed and is healing you?**

You can't control how other people respond to you. If they treat you differently, then it's their issue, not yours. All you can do is live healed, reassuring them by your life that you're on the path of restoration. It's your actions that'll reassure them that you're okay.

**Why is it that we victims feel ashamed of sharing our experience?**

Because sexual abuse involves sex—a very private act. Even though we live in a sex-crazed culture, most of us do not share about sex openly. It's simply not done. And some of us have a hard time giving ourselves grace because we believe we asked for it—or that if we share our story, the person listening will believe we deserved to be treated that way.

**After being married for 11 years, I still feel like I cannot enjoy my husband the way I should or want to as a result of years of sexual abuse from cousins, boyfriends and acquaintances. In our pre-marital counseling, our counselor mentioned that I did not have to share every detail of every situation since men are so visual. When I have brought up a situation or memory from my past that is still a**

**little painful, my husband feels like he "shouldn't have to pay for what somebody else did." He is loving and patient but it's hard for me to know what I should let him in on and what needs to stay between me and the Lord. Do you have any suggestions? As you have taken these steps of healing, have you shared everything with your husband or have you felt the need to use discretion on how much to share?**

It's okay to be specific as it pertains to you and your husband's sexual relationship. Even though it's unfair that your husband has to suffer for someone else's sin, he also doesn't want to do something that makes you remember the abuse. This is hard stuff. It's excruciating to say, "When you touch me there, I flash back." Perhaps instead of simply saying what not to do, share something positive too. Tell your husband what you like, or praise him for a particular way he loves you.

We are all visual beings, yes. You don't have to describe the exact act that a perpetrator did to you, only that something your spouse is doing is making you remember a terrible memory.

Also put yourself in his shoes. If you were doing something sexually that absolutely freaked him out or made him remember something traumatic, wouldn't you want to know?

In the process of healing, there will be times when the Lord shows you things or is working with you in your spirit. These are times when we often don't feel like sharing because it's too precious and tender. It's not fully formed. And that's okay to keep between you and God. "I'm not ready to share yet," is a good thing to say. And if there are things about your abuse that you aren't certain if you should share, ask God for guidance.

**How/when do you share abuse history when dating? I have significant physical injuries that aren't necessarily apparent outside of physical intimacy. I don't want to over-share, however I also don't want to blindside someone either.**

I shared my story with Patrick before we were engaged, but after he said, "I love you." Once I had a hunch that we might be engaged, I felt he needed to know. Still, I didn't even understand the extent of the damage. So telling doesn't prevent pain later, but it does pave the way for open communication right away.

**How did you come to terms with Jesus watching you while you were being abused?**

I talked a little about this in the honesty chapter. I still wrestle with this. I know all the theological answers, that God allows freewill to people who abuse others, but it's still hard for me to understand why God doesn't protect children. I've learned to look at this question differently in this latter phase of my healing—to trace the handprint of God in my life, to see how He did rescue me, to focus on the amazing amount of healing He has done in the aftermath. I also see Him grieving over me as a child, weeping alongside. And I remember that He bore the sins of those boys on the cross. He felt those sins.

## What books would you recommend for healing from the past?

*The Wounded Heart* by Dan Allender (and the accompanying workbook—one of the most foundational works about sexual abuse and the Christian).

*Changes that Heal* by Cloud and Townsend (very helpful in identifying dysfunctional patterns from the past and living free of them today).

*Thin Places* by Yours Truly (me!) (this tells my entire story up close and personal. I believe we all feel less alone when we share our stories).

*Boundaries* by Cloud and Townsend (another great book about establishing boundaries toward people who have constantly violated them. Remember, you cannot heal when you keep getting re-wounded. A boundary is necessary for your healing).

*Wishing on Dandelions* by Mary DeMuth (a good book to give to a teen who has been abused. It's a novel where the teenaged character has to face romantic love after carrying a terrible secret).

*As We Forgive* by Catherine Claire Larson (stories of forgiveness from the Rwandan genocide. A heart-stopping look at the power of forgiveness).

*Hinds' Feet on High Places* by Hannah Hurnard (an allegory of healing).

*When God Weeps* by Joni Earekson Tada (one of the most profound books about suffering and growth I've ever read).

*Til We Have Faces* by C.S. Lewis (another allegory that mirrors the healing journey).

*The Book of the Dun Cow* by Walter Wangerin (an amazing allegory about abuse and how we carry it with us into adulthood. Read and see if you can identify with Pertelote).

*Renewed: Finding Your Inner Happy in an Overwhelmed World* by Lucille Zimmerman (an entirely practical book written from a counselor's perspective about the practice of self care).

*Daring Greatly: How the Courage to Be Vulnerable Transforms the Way We Live, Love, Parent and Lead* by Brene Brown (all her books deal with this idea of embracing vulnerability, something very difficult for an abuse victim, but so important in the healing process).

*When a Man You Love Was Abused: A Woman's Guide to Helping Him Overcome Sexual Abuse* by Cec Murphey (also very instructive to men who have walked the road of sexual abuse).

# BONUS CHAPTER
# 2

# AN ANCIENT PATHWAY TO HEALING: THE LAMENT PSALM

Sometimes in the Christian community we shun grieving. We feel obligated to buck up, bury the pain, and put on an all-is-joy face. We expect ourselves to bounce back, stop questioning, and move on with our lives. Yet this doesn't work, does it? When I stay stuck in my pain, I've had to learn to refer back to David who wrote many of the Psalms. He is adept at grieving. He gives full bent to his complaints. He doesn't sugar-coat his anger, nor does he shrink back from sharing his questions or frustration.

There's a term for this type of written grieving: lament psalms. Lament psalms are an outcry against injustice, pain, and enemies inflicting harm. They are the tell-alls of the ancient world—the good, the bad, and certainly the ugly. For those of us who have walked through sexual abuse—who grow tired of people saying, "that was so long ago, why can't you get over it?"—learning to lament will help us move through the process of grief and get to the other side.

J. William Worden, a psychology professor at Harvard Medical University, in his study on grief has uncovered what he calls the "Tasks of Mourning" (which implies just how much hard work grief can be). The tasks are:

- Accept the reality of the loss.
- Access the pain of grief.
- Adjust to the new reality.
- Relocate the person you're grieving and move on.[40]

Obviously, this process refers to losing a loved one, but there are implications for sexual abuse victims. We must live in light of reality—not denying what happened, but acknowledging the full story. Though painful, we have to walk through the pain of the incident(s) in order to heal. We then can live in the new reality of a survivor of sexual abuse—as one who is no longer being abused. The last stage is trickier—since what we grieve is not the loss of a person, but the loss of innocence. We need to place the sexual abuse soundly in the past, perhaps on a shelf in our mind so we can live today instead of constantly tethered to the past. We can ask God to reframe the way we see the abuse, with an eye toward our redemptive story.

It's interesting to note that a lament psalm loosely follows these tasks of grief. A lament boasts a particular pattern—though not always in order. The main elements include:

- A complaint about a painful situation, or questions about why God doesn't seem to be helping.
- A confession of trust in God despite the current struggle.
- A request that God would act on your behalf.
- An offer to praise God in the midst of the pain.
- An assurance that God is in control.

A lament, essentially, is your pain intersecting with God's action. There are dozens of lament psalms, but several that deal with personal tragedy and pain.[41] Reading through the personal lament psalms, three stood out to me in terms of sexual abuse—Psalm 28, 31, and 43. Let's look at Psalm 43 for this structure:

### Psalm 43, NLT

*Declare me innocent, O God!*

*Defend me against these ungodly people.*

*Rescue me from these unjust liars.*

(A complaint about a painful situation, or questions about why God isn't helping.)

*For you are God, my only safe haven.*

(A confession of trust in God despite the current

struggle)

*Why have you tossed me aside?*

*Why must I wander around in grief,*

*oppressed by my enemies?*

(Another complaint about a painful situation, or questions about why God isn't helping.)

*Send out your light and your truth;*

*let them guide me.*

*Let them lead me to your holy mountain,*

*to the place where you live.*

(A request that God would act on your behalf.)

*There I will go to the altar of God,*

*to God—the source of all my joy.*

*I will praise you with my harp,*

*O God, my God!*

(An offer to praise God in the midst of the pain.)

*Why am I discouraged?*

*Why is my heart so sad?*

*I will put my hope in God!*

*I will praise him again—*

*my Savior and my God!*

(An assurance that God is in control.)

Consider the implications for you. When have you felt angry with God for what happened? Have you voiced that anger? Have you given yourself permission to complain? If David, the man known as the person after God's heart, can cry out, why can't you? God knows your pain already. Writing your own lament psalm is one simple way to begin your grief tasks.

To get you started, I'll share my lament psalm with you.

## MARY'S PSALM OF LAMENT

*Why, O Lord, didn't You intervene?*

*Why did You stand aloof when those boys stole so much from me?*

*I didn't know You then, but You knew me.*

*As my loving Father, why didn't You rescue?*

*Now that I have children, I don't understand.*

*If my children were being hurt, and I had the means to protect and save, I would.*

*Why didn't you punish those boys for what they did?*

*Why do they walk this earth, seemingly unharmed from the injury they inflicted?*

*What they did altered my identity.*

*Their actions undermined my innocence, made me feel unworthy, dirty, ashamed.*

*And I was only five years old.*

*They pinned me down.*

*They threatened death.*

*They hurt me.*

*And even when I told, no one in my life bothered to protect.*

*Those boys left me marked, so other predators could find me.*

*Their actions wounded me, made me walk life with a limp.*

*Their words made me grow up too soon, made me too wise to the things of this world.*

(A complaint about a painful situation, or questions about why God isn't helping.)

*But as I vent these very real questions, I also consider who I'd be without You.*

*Who would I go to other than to You to find healing?*

*You who understands violation.*

*You who shouldered every sexual sin upon the cross.*

*You who hung naked before a jeering crowd.*

(A confession of trust in God despite the current struggle)

*Would You please heal me?*

*Would You make me whole?*

*Would You help me experience sex as beautiful, as nurturing, as right?*

*Would You speak to those boys, now men, about what they did to me?*

*Would You give them grace as they grapple with what they did?*

*If it be Your will, could there be reconciliation there?*

(A request that God would act on your behalf.)

*Yes, God, I've been angry.*

*What I endured doesn't seem fair.*

*It seems like way too much for a child to bear.*

*But even so, I choose to rest in this truth: You are good.*

*I may not always understand Your ways.*

*I may not grasp Your protection.*

*I may not even like the path I've had to walk.*

*But I am small, and You are big.*

*You are sovereign.*

*You make good things come from evil.*

*So I rest there.*

*And I wait expectantly for You to transform this evil into something beautiful.*

(An offer to praise God in the midst of the pain.)

*It's not up to me to punish those boys.*

*It's not my responsibility to seek justice.*

*But I can offer forgiveness as You have forgiven me.*

*I can choose to relinquish my angst in Your capable hands.*

*I can believe You love this world.*

*You are God, and I am not.*

*Keep me trusting.*

*Amen.*

(An assurance that God is in control.)

Feel free to write as little or as much as you'd like. The lament psalm is a writing journey that moves you away from the anger over the violation to a healthy trust in God today. You may need to write one lament psalm, or you might have to pen twenty. I give you permission to scribble everything that's on your heart, no reservations. If it stays inside your head, the grief tangles. But there is freedom in getting the pain onto the page.

May it be that we learn the art of grieving well, letting go of all that bitterness, and embracing the great, wide, right now.

# APPENDIX
# 1

# PROTECT YOUR KIDS FROM SEXUAL ABUSE

Why do sexual predators prey on kids? Here is my unscientific list, born of my own experience.

**Because of opportunity and desire.**

Every crime committed needs these two elements. A perpetrator has to want to abuse, and there needs to be a victim in proximity. Usually a perpetrator has authority (older, a church leader, a parent, an adult) over the child and can use intimidation to keep the child silent. He may tell the child he'll kill her or her parents, or make up other horrifying reasons why the child must not tell. Because of their authority, and children are told to obey all authority, (and they're often bigger than their victim), the child complies.

## Because (often) they're acting out of their own difficult and unresolved past.

They may have been abused as children and now are flawed, broken people who haven't been brave enough to chase healing. Without working through the pain of their own abuse and finding health, they often (not always) can't help but abuse.

## Because we prefer to live in a culture of silence.

My babysitter chose to look the other way. For some of you, someone in authority chose not to think about the abuse; instead they covered it up, heaping shame upon shame, favoring the predator to the one preyed upon. In this cauldron of silence where no one is brought to task or judgment, abuse continues and flourishes.

## Because they (sometimes) can't meet their emotional needs in normal relationships.

Because of injury, they've learned the only way to get close to someone is to dominate and humiliate and coerce. They falsely believe this constitutes a personal relationship.

## Because there is power in getting away with a crime.

The statistics about perpetrators being brought to actual justice plays this out. Therefore, each subsequent victim fuels invincibility and a need to continue. After all, they won't (typically) be caught.

**Because they somehow believe that what they're doing isn't wrong.**

They've minimized the crime to something trivial, and therefore don't feel remorse. Or they rationalize their behavior. Pedophiles believe the child is consenting, or that they are "helping" the child by teaching them how to love. They are giving the child a "gift" of their own love. (This isn't always the case. I'm sure there are perpetrators who know what they're doing is wrong and feel tremendous guilt.)

**Because the perpetrator has dehumanized the victim in his/her mind.**

Instead of a child in need of protection and love, they've reduced the child to a vehicle for pleasure. This dehumanization can stem from mental disorders or violating their consciences over and over again until they believe those they abuse "deserve" it.

**Because perpetrators live and believe in hedonism, that everything and everyone exists for their pleasure.**

This is closely linked to narcissism. Those with extreme narcissistic tendencies (with narcissistic personality disorder) can't see beyond their own world, wants, and desires.

• • •

You'll notice that few of these reasons have to do with culture or society. While I have no doubt that our highly sexualized culture contributes to the problem, I believe the true issue is the heart. All abusive behavior flows from a hard heart, from one choice that leads to many, many choices until the conscience is seared and no longer in operation. Abuse thrives when we are silent, like the cover-ups in the clergy abuse scandals. It thrives under the guise of cronyism, where a system must be preserved at any cost, even if that cost means victims are ignored, silenced, or ridiculed.

Let's open the doors on this abuse, let the clean air and sunshine in. Let's tell the truth. For the sake of those abused and for the sake of the abusers. Covering it up doesn't help. Blaming external factors like society is short sighted. Being honest and realistic about the problem is the pathway toward healing.[42] At least that's one victim's thoughts.

In light of that, here are some things I've observed that may help you as you love and parent your kids, protecting them, yet still letting them be kids.

## KNOW YOUR CHILD.

The best defense in protecting your kids is knowing them well. Know their nuances; become a student of their behavior. In kindergarten when all hell swirled around me, I had a sudden change of behavior. A compliant child to a fault, I suddenly came home with a bad grade. Instead of asking questions and trying to figure out why a compliant child would morph to an uncooperative one, my parents scolded me.

If your child has a sudden shift in behavior, take it seriously. Become fascinated about his/her issues. Love her through it. Chances are it won't be because of a sexual predator, but knowing your child's heart in any situation will only deepen your relationship.[43]

**Some symptoms of sexual abuse include:**

- Sudden problems at school—with either withdrawal or behavior problems
- Fear of you leaving them—being clingy or crying when you drop your child off somewhere
- Nightmares or night terrors
- Insomnia
- Incontinence, including sudden bedwetting and frequent urinary tract infections
- Physical evidence (bleeding)
- Sudden change in eating patterns (stops eating, eats too much)
- Self harm (head banging, cutting, drug abuse)
- An extreme need to be perfect
- Fear of one particular person
- Onset of depression and/or suicidal thoughts
- Inappropriate sexual touch of themselves or others

## BE VIGILANT BUT NOT IMMOBILIZED.

Be cautious about adults seeking alone time with your child. Watch your children and who they hang out with at the park, at church, in the neighborhood. Also be careful in church. Know the choir director, Awana leader, Sunday School teacher. Observe the ministry; offer to assist.

Remember that abusers seldom look like criminals or creeps. They often appear trustworthy and upstanding. Predators operate by getting kids (and often parents) to trust them. They offer gifts. They seem to love like Jesus does—to an extreme extent. They spend lots of time with kids, and work hard at currying favor with them.

There's a tension here, though. Don't become so immobilized that you never let your kids be kids. You don't want to raise a fear-based child. Still, trust your instincts.

## TEACH YOUR KIDS ABOUT SEX

Because of the overwhelming proliferation of pornography on the internet,[44] you'll need to talk about sex with your kids at an early age—in an age-appropriate manner. We let our kids' questions lead our discussions. So if a child wants to know where babies came from, we shared in a matter-of-fact way—with accurate terms for parts of the sexual anatomy. We tried to speak frankly and without embarrassment—not an easy thing to do, but important if you want to have open discussion and keep sex in the arena of normal conversation. The more you're comfortable with talking about it, the more comfortable your kids will be in bringing you any concerns.

When you talk about sex, remember to talk about what is appropriate, safe touch and what is off limits. As you talk with your children about this, remind them that they have every right to say no, and say it with conviction. Tell them they can talk to you if they ever feel uncomfortable in someone else's presence. In the pre-teen years, let them know that perpetrators will use threats—that they might even say things like, "I'll kill you if you tell." Remind them that perpetrators love to lie about everything, and that their threats often don't have teeth.

In our Christian homes in particular, our children are taught to obey those in authority over them. But we must also teach them that it is appropriate to say no if they're feeling shame or pressure—or they're experiencing unwanted touch. Tell them you'd rather them err on the side of caution (and saying too many "nos") than worry about disappointing an adult.

In talking about sex, discuss secrets—that having secrets about someone hurting your child—should be told. Any secret that makes a child feel icky or ashamed is a secret that must be told.

## ENTRUST YOUR KIDS TO JESUS.

Often I hear parents ask me if I have danced over the line into hyper-vigilance with my kids in other areas of their lives. Although I have warned them about stranger danger and how to flee, and we've talked about inappropriate touch, I have also learned to entrust my kids to Jesus. We need to be careful of falling into what I call "The Cult of Protectionism," protecting their kids at any cost, never letting their children expand, grow, explore. We can lean toward controlling our kids, micromanaging their worlds. While we should protect our kids, we're also role models, demonstrating a life lived in adventure, not fear. If we insulate our kids from every perceived harm, how will they experience their own adventure?

Pray for and with your children. Tell them about sex and unwanted touch. Warn them about predators. Empower their "no" muscle. Realize that we live in a fallen, broken world.

No matter how vigilant we are, we can't protect them from everything. And God doesn't always protect them either, which is hard to swallow, hard to work through. I wish I could promise that if we pray and protect and warn, no harm will befall our dear kids. What we can do is create a haven-like home where our kids feel protected and free to share their lives with us. We can foster an environment of truth and authenticity where our kids know they can entrust us with their secrets.

## OUR GREATEST GIFT

The greatest gift we can give your kids is our relationship with Jesus, modeling to them what we do when we're injured or hurt. Our own willingness to run to Him with our pain will show our kids how to work through their own difficulties as they grow up. Contagious family life is not about appearing perfect, or being the model Christian family. It's not about covering up our messes. It's about a bunch of messy people living together, broken, but running to Jesus for healing and help.[45]

# APPENDIX
# 2

# THE ORIGINAL POST
# THAT STARTED THIS

I sat in the audience, taking notes, my heart sinking deeper into itself. Failure hollered so loudly I wondered if others could hear it. Women laughed, turned red-faced, then laughed some more. I sat quiet, alone with my condemnation.

The woman at the front of the conference talked about sex, about being a hottie for your honey. She spoke of livening up the marriage bed, that God made sex to be amazing, fulfilling. That it was our duty to make it a joy, to lavish our husbands with our sexuality. Maybe he could eat strawberries from our bellies, or we could sneak little hot notes to him.

I looked around the room, wondering if I was the only one who felt unable to do any of these acts. I felt like a skinny girl sitting in on a sumo wrestling seminar, wholly incapable of carrying out the tips and tricks offered.

I remembered the statistics, that most likely a large swath of these laughing women had been sexually assaulted at one point in their lives. That as I listened to the speaker share her story, fifteen people had experienced unwanted sexual touch (one every two minutes).

And then I got mad. It was one of the first times I'd ever considered interrupting a speaker. But of course, there were hundreds of women, and they were laughing, listening, making sexy lists, and engaging.

If I'd had the gumption, this is what I would've said: "Could you please address those of us who find this impossible? Please don't place yet another yoke upon us. We're just trying to work through the past, barely able to understand sex as 'beautiful.' To many of us, it's dirty, and it serves as a constant reminder that we were violated against our will."

Have you ever felt this way? Am I the lone voice calling out to adventurous spouses who don't at all struggle with this? When my husband and I wrote an article for *Marriage Partnership* about the marriage bed and past sexual abuse, the response was overwhelming, so I'm guessing I'm not writing to an empty internet here.

When I speak one on one with people who have been sexually abused, a great majority of them have a difficult time with sex. They either border on addiction or have sworn off sex entirely (even in marriage). Some divorce because they simply cannot have sex with their spouse. It's a real problem, but so few talk about it.

My own story and journey of healing is chronicled in my memoir *Thin Places*. I was molested at five years old during my kindergarten career by neighborhood bullies, who eventually brought their friends in on the violation. I told my babysitter. She said she'd tell my mom (but never did), and the boys continued to violate me, which led me to believe that not one adult on earth would protect me. I grew a fierce determination to protect myself, so I feigned sleep to get out of the attacks. Providentially, we moved at the end of that year, far enough away from those boys that I didn't have to endure their violation any more.

But boy did they stay with me. They haunted my dreams. They obscured my view of sex. They made me think that my sole purpose in this life was to be used and violated.

I don't know how I was able to walk the aisle of marriage a virgin—it's truly God's grace. Technically, of course, I wasn't. All those violations from the past ensured that. But when it became my choice, I found the strength to say no.

Truth be told, I walked a strange line between yearning and utter terror. As a fatherless girl, I wanted nothing more than to have a boyfriend fill up all the empty spaces of me, but when my love interest became interested, I ran one thousand miles away, completely terrified. I worried they'd try to make me do things I didn't ever want to do.

When I got engaged, I worried a lot about sex. My wedding night was not something I anticipated with joy or expectation. The terror refrained inside me. I felt five again.

I shared those fears with my husband, and we made it through. And I'm frankly quite surprised (it is the gift of God) that I can enjoy sex.

But it's taken many years over the past twenty-two to get to a healthy place. I still disconnect. I can't seem to engage my emotions or my whole self. If I enjoy sex, I still have the feeling that I'm legitimizing the abuse. I've come to a place of acceptance, too, that I may never be the sexy wife who is "all that" for her husband. My growth has been tremendous, but I still have scars.

We've learned to talk about it, not an easy thing to do. My husband knows I'm trying, that I'm not giving up. I've been able to communicate my triggers to him, which has helped a lot.

And through it all, I honestly have to cry out to Jesus to give me a healthy view of sex. It absolutely does not come naturally to me. My fallback is revulsion.

All this stinks. It's not fair that those boys stole the most precious part of me. It's not fair to me, and it's not fair to my husband. They violated, and I'm left to navigate the minefield of memories and feelings.

I walk with a giant limp in the sexy wife arena. I still feel outright rage when I read that for the sake of my husband, I'm supposed to be adventurous and wild, that to be this way represents true spousal godliness. Because honestly? Those words just make me feel less than. Those are a set of guidelines I'll probably never meet.

I haven't given up. I press on to be whole. But I also know my limitations. And I know that many of you are reading this and saying, yes, yes. Mind if I offer you grace?

It's okay to struggle in this area. It's normal. I give you permission to say it's frightening and bewildering. I pray you'll find the words to communicate with your spouse how you feel, how this is hard for you. I hope for an understanding spouse who loves you utterly for who you are, not how you perform. I want to tell you that it does get better, but that you won't improve by simply trying to on sexy clothes or offering your body as a fruit plate. True sexual liberation comes from the inside out, where Jesus walks into those terrible memories and mourns alongside you. I don't have the answers. I still can't reconcile my own sexual exploitation with a loving God, other than to say He has used those awful events to make me more empathetic to those who have walked similar paths. And the thrill that comes when I'm able to offer words of encouragement and truth salves the wound a bit. Whether you're a man or a woman, hear this: You are beautiful. You are worthy of being cherished. You are worth healing. Stay on the course. Holler your anger if you have to. But keep asking Jesus for healing. And keep offering grace to fellow strugglers.

# 10 WAYS TO SHARE THE NOT MARKED MESSAGE

If you've been impacted by the message of this book and would like to help other sexual abuse victims find healing, here are some specific ways you can be a part.

1. Like *Not Marked* on Facebook. Facebook.com/ NotMarked

2. Tweet about *Not Marked* using this hashtag: #NotMarked

3. Visit www.NotMarked.com and share the site.

4. Contact sexual abuse recovery ministries on Mary's behalf. Use this email when introducing them: mary@marydemuth.com.

5. Buy the book in bulk and give it to those who may need it, including sex-trafficking ministries, prisons, counseling centers. Purchase in bulk at a discount at www. NotMarked.com.

6. Ask Mary and/or Mary and Patrick to speak about sexual abuse recovery. Click here to book: http://www.marydemuth.com/speaking-topics/

7. Host Mary on your blog or Facebook page. Email her at mary@marydemuth.com
8. Ask bookstores to stock *Not Marked*.
9. Start a revolution of book lending kindness. Pass *Not Marked* onto a friend, then ask them to do the same when they're done.
10. The best way a book sells is by simple word of mouth. Talk about *Not Marked* with people who may benefit from its message.

# ENDNOTES

## Introduction

1. See Appendix Two for the original post.
2. Buchanan, Mark, *The Rest of God.* (Nashville: Thomas Nelson 2006) 150.
3. http://www.sticypress.org/about-us-st-irenaeus. nxg
4. Most sexual abuse survivors don't dare to stick a toe into the tunnel. The fact that you're reading this book means you have. You're tired of living the way you've lived. You're sick of the triggers when you have sex (if you can have sex at all). You're tired of feeling used, dirty, and shameful when you participate in sex. You're wary of all those years of living a lie, pretending to do an act without actually connecting to the moment. You want to be fully alive, so you stuck your toe in when you opened the pages of *Not Marked*. I wholeheartedly and joyfully commend you. And as one who has placed toe, leg, torso, heart, and mind into the tunnel and lived to tell about it from the vista of the

other side, let me say simply this: it's worth it. If you're afraid, it's normal. But your bravery in wanting to get well is the first step (even if you feel trepidation with your toe in the darkness).

5. See http://www.nimh.nih.gov/health/publications/post-traumatic-stress-disorder-ptsd/index.shtml for a discussion of this and a listing of symptoms.

6. Getting to that place where you can share sometimes feels overwhelming. Our past feels too heavy, too much—and daring to share it borders on impossibility.

## Chapter 1

7. From the hymn "O the Deep Deep Love of Jesus" http://en.wikipedia.org/wiki/O_the_Deep,_Deep_Love_of_Jesus

## Chapter 3

8. See my book *Building the Christian Family You Never Had* (Colorado Springs, CO: Waterbrook Multnomah Publishing Group 2005) Chapter 7.

9. If you'd like to do further study, check out *Honor Thy Father and Mother: Filial Responsibility in Jewish Law and Ethics* by Gerald J. Bildstein, particularly pages 130–136. (KATV Publishing House 2006).

10. Stoop, David, *Forgiving Our Parents, Forgiving Ourselves: Healing Adult Children of*

*Dysfunctional Families* (Grand Rapids: Regal Publishing 2011) 291.

11. Lamott, Anne, *Bird by Bird: Some Instructions on Writing and Life* (New York, NY: Anchor Books 1994) Read the chapter, "The Moral Point of View."

12. Zimmerman, Lucille *Renewed: Finding Your Inner Happy in an Overwhelmed World* (Nashville, TN: Abingdon Press, 2013) 86.

13. Cloud, Dr. Henry and Townsend, John. *Changes that Heal: How to Understand Your Past to Ensure a Healthier Future* (Grand Rapids, MI: Zondervan 1993) 47.

14. Brown, Brene: *Daring Greatly: How the Courage to Be Vulnerable Transforms the Way We Live, Love, Parent and Lead* (New York, NY: Gotham Books 2013) 82.

15. Pennebaker, James: *Writing to Heal: A Guided Journal for Recovering from Trauma and Emotional Upheaval* (Oakland: New Harbinger Publications 2004).

16. Brown, Brene: *Daring Greatly: How the Courage to Be Vulnerable Transforms the Way We Live, Love, Parent and Lead* (New York, NY: Gotham Books 2013) 33.

## Chapter 5

17. For a thorough explanation, read *EMDR Eye Movement Desensitization & Reprocessing: The Breakthrough "Eye Movement" Therapy*

*for Overcoming Anxiety, Stress and Trauma* by Francine Shapiro, Ph D and Margot Silk Forrest.

## Chapter 6

18. http://www.brainyquote.com/quotes/quotes/u/ursulakle132606.html
19. Gire, Ken, *Windows of the Soul: Experiencing God in New Ways* (Grand Rapids, MI: Zondervan, 1996).
20. Niequist, Shauna Bittersweet: *Thoughts on Change, Grace, and Learning the Hard Way* (Grand Rapids, MI: Zondervan 2010) 160.
21. http://www.artsaftercare.org
22. *Watching the Tree Limbs* (CreateSpace).

## Chapter 8

23. http://psychiatry.ubc.ca/person/rosemary-basson/
24. http://www.psychologytoday.com/blog/all-about-sex/200907/desire-in-women-does-it-lead-sex-or-result-it also http://www.psychologytoday.com/blog/all-about-sex/201204/which-comes-first-desire-or-sex

## Chapter 9

25. Larson, Catherine Claire, *As We Forgive: Stories of Reconciliation from Rwanda* (Grand Rapids, MI: Zondervan, 2009).

**Chapter 10**

26. DeMuth, Mary, *Everything: What You Give and What You Gain to Become Like Jesus.* (Nashville, Thomas Nelson Publishers, 2012) pages 65–74.

27. Buchanan, Mark, *The Rest of God* (Nashville, TN: Thomas Nelson, 2007) 209–210.

**Chapter 11**

28. Chambers, Oswald, *My Utmost for His Highest* (Westwood, NJ: Barbour and Company, 1935) 49.

29. Loehr, Jim, *The Power of Story: Change Your Story, Change Your Destiny in Business and in Life* (New York, NY: Free Press 2007) 14.

30. Niequist, Shauna *Bittersweet: Thoughts on Change, Grace, and Learning the Hard Way* (Grand Rapids, MI: Zondervan 2010) 17.

31. Buechner, Frederick. *Wishful Thinking: A Seeker's ABC* (San Francisco, CA: Harper SanFrancisco 1993) 39.

**Bonus Chapter One**

32. Zimmerman, Lucille *Renewed: Finding Your Inner Happy in an Overwhelmed World* (Nashville, TN: Abingdon Press, 2013) 52.

33. See this article for a thorough investigation about recidivism rates for sex offenders. http://www.corrections.com/news/article/24500-facts-and-fiction-about-sex-offenders

34. Patrick talks about the book and my healing. http://www.notmarked.com

35. Here's one: http://www.news.harvard.edu/gazette/2006/10.12/01-abuse.html

36. A Public Statement Concerning Sexual Abuse in the Church of Jesus Christ. http://netgrace.org/a-public-statement-concerning-sexual-abuse-in-the-church-of-jesus-christ/

37. http://www.marydemuth.com/bonnets-buggies-and-sexual-abuse/

38. DeMuth, Mary, *The Wall Around Your Heart: How Jesus Heals You When Others Hurt You* (Nashville, TN: Thomas Nelson Publishers 2013).

39. http://netgrace.org/a-public-statement-concerning-sexual-abuse-in-the-church-of-jesus-christ/

## Bonus Chapter Two

40. http://psychcentral.com/lib/grief-healing-and-the-one-to-two-year-myth/000375

41. http://www.xenos.org/classes/psalms/psweek2.htm has a listing of different types of lament psalms. This would make an interesting personal study.

## Appendix One

42. This is a great article about the truth about sexual abuse and how to protect your kids: http://www.pandys.org/articles/protectyourchild.html

43. Here's a listing of typical abuse symptoms: http://www.speakingout-csa.com/signssymptoms.html

44. Eye-opening report about how pornography affects our kids. (Trigger alert). http://www.dailymail.co.uk/femail/article-2432591/Experiment-convinced-online-porn-pernicious-threat-facing-children-today-By-ex-lads-mag-editor-MARTIN-DAUBNEY.html

45. For a book-long discussion on this kind of family life, pick up my book, *You Can Raise Courageous and Confident Kids* (Eugene, OR: Harvest House Publishers, 2011).

# ACKNOWLEDGEMENTS

To the readers who encouraged me to write this book, thank you. I revisited the pain from the past for your sake. I pray this book blesses you.

This book had a unique pathway to publication—via a crowdfunding effort that both worried and blessed me. I hoped to raise enough to publish this book, but the response was so overwhelming, we ended up having enough capital to produce two bonus chapters, a study guide, two webinars and an audio book. A huge thank you to Thomas Umstattd of Author Media who shepherded me through the month-long Indiegogo campaign. Your guidance and advice was in direct proportion to our success.

Thank you to the 501 people who helped fund this book, I truly don't know how to say thank you. Your support and comments meant everything to me. These donors supported at the "Name Bird" level, which means they get a special shout out here. Laurie Wallin, D'Shon Berry, Barbara Ridlington, Suzanne Snydar, Dave Anthold, Amy Smith, Kristin Early, Charissa Giesbrecht, Winning Kids Inc., Sundi Jo Graham, Sharilyn A. Ross, Dr. Angie Welikala, David

Hernandez, and Sharon Sattler Pfost, thank you for believing in this book!

To my prayer team: this book's success is the result of your many prayers. We've been together nearly a decade now, and look at what God has wrought! Big hugs to Twilla, Renee, Carla, Caroline, Cheramy, Jeanne, D'Ann, Dorian, Erin, Ginger, Helen, Holly, Jen, Kathy, Katy G., Katy R., Denise, Anita, Diane, Cyndi, Lesley, Leslie, Liz, Marcia, Marion, Marybeth, Pam, Paula, Phyllis, Becky, Sandi, Sarah, Tim, Tina, Tracy, John, Nicole, Tosca, Marilyn, TJ, Patrick, Jody, Susan, Ariel, Mary, Amy, Lisa, Dena, Carol, Kathryn, Esther, Susie, Christy, Kimberly, Jodi, Ericka, Denise, Alice, Randy, Paul, Jan, Sophie, Sarah, Michele, Judy, Thomas, Heidi, Aldyth, Teresa, Christy and Sue.

To the DeMuth Advisory Board, thank you for walking me through this project and offering wise counsel. You're right—I'm not the "sexual abuse lady" but an ambassador of healing—by God's grace. Thanks to Patrick, Pam, Thomas, Randy, Alice, Heidi, Kimberly, Denise, Holly, Leslie, D'Ann, Jody, Cathleen, Esther and Sandi.

To my agent, Esther Fedorkevich: Wow. Your constant and steadfast belief in me stuns me every time. Your words of encouragement always arrive at the perfect time—when Debbie Downer threatens to take over.

To my editor, Lissa Halls Johnson, you've made this book so much better. Thank you for your keen editorial eye, but more than that, thanks for your heart behind the edits.

Patrick, I am grateful for your words in this book—our first venture together. Thank you for being so patient. We've weathered difficult storms, but we've emerged as best friends and the sweetest of lovers. I love you.

Sophie, Aidan, and Julia, thank you for supporting me in this difficult book, I know it can't be easy knowing I walked through all this. You represent redemption to me. May you walk into adulthood wildly dedicated to Jesus and His kingdom.

Jesus, thank You for healing me. For erasing the mark. For setting my feet upon a rock so I can declare Your message of redemption to many. It's all for You. You get the glory for my story.